George Herbert

Neil Curry and Natasha Curry

GREENWICH EXCHANGE
LONDON

Greenwich Exchange, London

George Herbert
©Neil Curry and Natasha Curry 2009

First published in Great Britain in 2010
All rights reserved

Printed and bound by **imprint**digital.net
Typesetting and layout by Jude Keen, London
Tel: 020 8355 4541
Cover design by December Publications, Belfast
Tel: 028 90286559
Cover image: George Herbert ©Mary Evans Picture Library
Back cover author image: Courtesy of Kai Bansner

Greenwich Exchange Website: www.greenex.co.uk

Cataloguing in Publication Data is available from the
British Library.

ISBN-13: 978-1-906075-40-8

for *Kai*

Contents

1

The Life

"a lifeline to God ..."

George Herbert, self-declared pacifist, creator of some of the most passionate religious poems, actually came from a long line of warriors and battle-decorated fighters. The tales of heroism along the male family line are legendary: his great-great-grandfather is said to have fought his way "through a whole army and back again"; his father walked valiantly home after his skull had been split open by "adversaries"; one of his brothers overcame his opponent with a broken sword, and yet another took command of a ship in the East Indies and forced the Spanish fleet into submission all the while allegedly suffering from twenty-four stab wounds himself. George Herbert, sickly and virtually penniless throughout a great deal of his life, lean to an extremity, as we are told, fought a different battle – a battle between his devotion to God, and his enduring feelings of spiritual inadequacy.

This was by all accounts a remarkable family. Herbert's father was descended from one of the oldest and most powerful families in Wales, and could trace his line back to the early thirteenth century. Through calculated marriages, and a long history of public service, the Herbert line established itself as a political and financial force to be reckoned with.

Richard Herbert, Lord of Cherbury and of Montgomery Castle, was a Justice of the Peace, Sheriff and Parliamentarian. He fathered ten children, seven boys and three girls, then died suddenly when young George was only three and a half years old, and while his brother Thomas was still to be born. Herbert may have grown up in a Reformation version of a single-parent household, but his mother Magdalen was an extraordinary woman and the arrival among all these warriors and politicians of two poets and men of intellect – George and his elder brother Edward – in one generation, must owe much to the changes in the gene pool provided by her. She proved more than capable of managing the family's financial and business affairs, and overseeing the spiritual and academic development of her children. In an age when many families lost some or all of their children in infancy and childhood, Magdalen brought all ten to adulthood.

Reports of the Herbert household describe it as a lively, high-spirited environment. The metaphysical poet John Donne, a frequent visitor, remembered the house as "a court, in the conversation of the best." While prayer and religious contemplation were clearly at the centre of their day, the children are said to have been expert archers, equestrians, and musicians; the only activity forbidden to them was swimming as their mother claimed to have "heard of more drowned than saved by it". Seldom were the Herberts without guests at meals. According to a household journal, *Kitchin Booke*, kept by Magdalen's steward John Gorse, the frequent entertainers included musicians, morris dancers, and "a blynde harper and his boys." Many a night was spent playing cards and while Magdalen played a tight hand, it is said that on one occasion she had to send for Gorse to help clear her debts for the evening.

Herbert was devoted to his mother, and many of his early works are either dedicated to, or inspired by, her:

> To thee I owe my birth of earth
> To thee I owe my heavenly birth
> As thou didst lead I followed thee;
> Thou wast a mother twice to me.

Twice mother in the fact that Magdalen gave birth to Herbert's physical and spiritual life, and yet possibly because she was both mother *and* father to the young boy.

Some years after her first husband's death, when Magdalen was forty, she married Sir John Danvers, the only father Herbert would ever know, and someone with whom he was to become extremely close. Magdalen had quite a catch in Sir John; he was half her age, had long flowing hair, and was said to stop foot traffic in Europe as people craned their necks to catch sight of his beauty. Despite the curious match, and the disapproval of the oldest son Edward, this was a happy marriage. Donne's comment: "she had a cheerfulness agreeable to his youth and he a sober staidness comfortable to her more years." And Donne's thoughts on the age difference: "I would put their years into one number and think them 30 apiece."

Magdalen educated her children at home for the first years of their life, along with a number of guest speakers and visiting scholars, according to Gorse's meticulous note-taking. However, it came time for Herbert to experience an education outside of the home. Magdalen had moved her family to Oxford, so as to be close to her eldest son Edward and his bride, then took a house in Charing Cross, still with Edward and his family in tow. So it was at the age of twelve, young George Herbert joined the other boys at Westminster as a day student under the watchful eye of the distinguished biblical scholar Lancelot Andrews, dean of the school and later named as Bishop of Chichester. One year later, most likely sponsored by Andrews, Herbert won a scholarship to the school, and boarded there along with forty other prestigious King's Scholars. The scholarship entailed a sort of 'academic hazing', in which aspiring scholars challenged each other in Latin and Greek translations, hoping for a stumble or misspoken word. This could last for as many as twelve weeks, and biographers have written of the severe "strain on the intellect, nerves and health of the candidates": these boys were between twelve and fifteen years old.

Herbert must have found academic and spiritual life at Westminster School somewhat familiar, as it was run along the same lines as his mother's household, although most likely without the morris dancers. Boys were allowed only two meals a day; dinner and supper in summer, lunch and dinner in winter. The overarching goal was to produce young men who were "pious, learned, gentlemanly and industrious," according to the school's statutes written in 1560. Young Herbert would have been rigorously schooled in Greek, Latin, rhetoric and Anglican piety. We learn of his distaste for exercise, and for time in the playground; he apparently took more interest in the "annual performances of the Latin Play". As the school was part of Westminster Abbey, all the King's Scholars attended church regularly and were expected to write up a detailed report of the sermon. Lancelot Andrews, known as "an angel in the pulpit", was an ideal ecclesiastical role model for the young Herbert.

Herbert was to continue his education at either Oxford or Cambridge, and, as a King's Scholar, had the chance of attending either Christ Church Oxford, or Trinity College Cambridge. Trinity it was, and Herbert began his studies there in 1609, under the mastership of Dr. Thomas Nevil, a renowned academic, and distinguished man of the church.

Cambridge in the 17th century had a tendency to make people ill, due to the muggy air that rose up from the fens. And it wasn't long before the hardworking Herbert had also fallen ill, a sickness, possibly tuberculosis, that was to plague him through most of the rest of his life, and which he feared might interfere with his studies and writing, "I fear the heat of my ague hath dried up those springs, by which the scholars say, the Muses use to take up their habitations," he wrote in a letter to his mother.

Students at Trinity in 1609 sound surprisingly like those of today. "Swearing, drinking and rioting" were not uncommon; dogs were forbidden, but students kept them for hunting. Bills for dancing lessons have also been noted among the students' papers, even though dancing school was forbidden.

There are few if any tales of Herbert's life as a student, except for reports of his refusal to conform to the expected monastic dress code, and a preference for clothes that "seemed to prove that he put too great a value on his parts and parentage". It also sounds as though he may have been a little overly proud of his family status: "He kept himself too much retired, and at too great a distance with all his inferiors."

Herbert was awarded his BA by 1613, and his MA by 1616. As a Master of Arts and a Trinity fellow, Herbert was expected to teach the undergraduates. He taught the course in Greek grammar, and was rapidly promoted to be the teacher of rhetoric across the entire university, an honour held by few before him. However, teaching was merely a sideline for his true passion: the study of divinity to which Herbert devoted his waking hours, ignoring the advice of his headmaster Dr Richard Ireland who cautioned, "study moderately and use exercise", and advised his students "not to impair their health with too much study."

Again, like students of today, Herbert soon found his reading list longer than his budget could manage: too many books, not enough money. Story has it that he would regularly choose books over food, and wrote many a letter to his family asking for his allowance to be doubled to allow him to be able to afford the books he needed. In a letter to his stepfather he wrote, "I am scarce able with much ado to make one half years allowance, shake hands with the other: And yet if a Book of four or five Shillings come in my way, I buy it, though I fast for it; yea, sometimes of Ten Shillings. But, alas Sir, what is that to those infinite Volumes of Divinity, which yet every day swell, and grow bigger." He made a convincing argument, and his family did their best to help him out, sending books and small amounts of money when they could; but Herbert was barely able to make a dent in the canon on his paltry salary.

We can only imagine Herbert's excitement when he was offered a position that would nearly double his annual income to £30 a year; let us remember that, even a century later, Goldsmith's village preacher was "passing rich with forty pounds a year". The position of Public Orator of Cambridge can be compared to a seventeenth-century public relations officer, charged with writing all the university's letters, public speaking, and generally networking on behalf of the university. Sir Francis Nethersole, the outgoing officer, apparently expressed some concerns that appointing Herbert to this position might hamper his studies in divinity, but we are told that Herbert pursued this post with his characteristic single-minded determination, "working the heads" like a born politician, convinced that he could carry out his civic duties in the glory of God. On 20th January, 1620, George Herbert was elected Public Orator of Cambridge University.

Thus followed a number of years of public service, during which time Herbert was introduced at court, socialized with nobles and aristocrats, and earned the favour of King James. As one biographer puts it, Herbert was wooed with "the painted pleasures, the glittering gauds of the world". The next logical step was to follow in his family's well-worn footsteps and serve in parliament.

A number of Herbert biographers have suggested that he turned his back on his devotional studies at this time, and on one of his obligations as a Trinity Fellow to take holy orders. Others imply that Herbert was only doing what was expected of him, given that no other male Herbert was available at the time to defend the family seat of Montgomery. Writing now, close to 400 years later, we'll never really know. What we do know is that Herbert requested a six-month sabbatical from Trinity College, and was readying himself for the next meeting of Parliament.

This was a turbulent time in English politics. The Thirty Years War was raging on the continent, war with Spain looked increasingly likely, a schism had widened between the puritan Church of Scotland and the Church of England, and freedom of worship for English Catholics was a contentious issue both at home and abroad.

Herbert's sentiments were aligned with the pacifist James I, and against the war mongering of his son Prince Charles. When the King died in 1625, Herbert must have known his future as a public servant was over. Records show that Herbert attended parliament only once in 1624, and shortly after declared his intention to be ordained as a deacon, which closed the door permanently on his "court hopes". Theories abound as to this seemingly abrupt career switch. Was it the death of his patron James I? Was it the militaristic nature of Charles' parliament? Or, most likely, had Herbert been planning a life of orders all along, and regarded his parliamentary life as a mere detour?

London in 1625 was wretched with the plague, and was not considered a fit place for a gentleman such as Herbert to live. He therefore left town and stayed with various friends, including his mother at Danvers House, where he would have spent time conversing with John Donne, a frequent visitor. Donne was then Dean of St Paul's, and one of England's most revered preachers, and it is said that he would use his time at Danvers House revising and rehearsing his sermons to this eager audience. Another regular guest was Nicholas Ferrar, the founder of the Little Gidding community who was also ordained in 1626, just a year before Herbert. If he hadn't been seriously contemplating taking orders before he moved to Danvers House, the influence of his mother, Donne and Ferrar must have done a lot to affirm his vocation. George Herbert had begun the journey towards ordination.

Herbert had caught the eye of the Bishop of Lincoln, John Williams, who bestowed upon him the sinecure at Llandinam, Montgomery a hamlet only a few miles from Herbert's birthplace, and eighteen months later made him canon of Lincoln Cathedral. Herbert flinched at the last offer, feeling strongly that it was undeserved, and tried to pass it off to his friend Ferrar. Ferrar, sensing the struggle Herbert was going through, refused, but suggested that some of the income from the canonship go towards renovating the nearby church of Leighton Bromswold, not far from the Little Gidding community. Not surprisingly, Herbert threw himself into the task "as though it were a lifeline to God".

His mother was far from pleased with these developments, and sent for her son advising him that it was not fitting for a man with his "weak body, and empty purse, to undertake to build churches". Herbert is said to have requested that "she would allow him, at thirty-three years, to become an undutiful son". Magdalen was known to have later contributed significantly to the restoration fund. The work at Leighton Bromswold was not finished until after Herbert's death, and it is not known if Herbert ever set foot in the church itself.

The following years saw a decline in Herbert's overall health. Between 1627 and 1628 he moved to the house of his brother, Sir Henry, in Essex where he claimed to cure his sickness by "forbearing to drink, and not eating any meat, no not mutton, nor a hen, or pigeon, unless they were salted".

This was a period in Herbert's life that was marked by death and loss. He was to lose his long-time friend Lancelot Andrews, former dean of Westminster, his close friend Sir Francis Bacon, and tragically his beloved mother, all within a very short time frame. Magdalen had lived into her mid-sixties, a great age for this period, yet story tells us that her last years were plagued with depression, possibly due to the untimely deaths of her son and daughter, and her husband's financial struggles with the Virginia Company. She was buried in the parish church close to Danvers House, but her funeral was delayed for close to three weeks so Donne would be able to deliver the sermon. Donne eulogized Magdalen, praising her as the best wife, "the best mother, the best neighbour, the best friend, the best example." Her son too published a collection of nineteen memorial poems, both in Latin and Greek, entitled *Memoriae Matris Sacrum.* At the end of this collection Herbert vows never to publish another poem:

> Driven by a fierce scourge, I've been unable to refuse
> Mother's great honor demands song.
> Alas I must write. You've conquered, O Muse! But listen,
> Foolish one, I write this one time that I may ever silent be.

And indeed, no further works were published during his lifetime.

Following his mother's death Herbert was granted lands in Worcestershire, and now finally had significant funds of his own for the first time in his life. He quickly gave up his oratorship, and went to live with his stepfather's brother, Henry Danvers, Earl of Danby, at Dauntsey House in Wiltshire. This was a rural household, more rural than anything Herbert had known, and gave him the space to ride his beloved horse, walk through the countryside, and the time for intense self and spiritual reflection. Herbert had spent years perfecting his public self, this was a time when his struggles with loss, inadequacy in the face of God, and anguish about how far he had come from his goal of devoting his life to God surfaced in his poetry:

> To have my aim, and yet to be
> Further from it when I bent my bow.

It is thought that over half the poems of his collection *The Temple* were written while Herbert was living at Dauntsey House.

In his poem 'The Thanksgiving', Herbert had written:

> I will not marry; or, if she be mine,
> She and her children shall be Thine.

Yet it wasn't long until he had taken Jane Danvers to be his wife, claiming that a choice of wife "was made rather by his ear, than by his eye." Jane was a cousin of Herbert's stepfather, John Danvers, and biographers have claimed that they were married within three days of meeting. Whatever the story, this was to prove a happy marriage, one built around pious devotion and a willingness to help others in the community. Early in 1630, Herbert was offered a dual parish, the Parish of Fugglestone St Peter, and the Chapel of Bemerton St Andrew. It was a large rural parish near Salisbury, mainly with a farming community, and the newlyweds moved into Bemerton rectory, which apparently was in need of extensive repair.

The Herberts never had children of their own, but when his sister Margaret died, he opened his home to her daughters, Dorothy and Magdalen, and enlisted them in his ministrations throughout the community. Although none of his sermons was ever printed, we are told that Herbert's first sermon at Bemerton was one of learned rhetoric and academic wit, the like of which would have better suited his position as Cambridge Orator. In all likelihood, this baffled his parishioners, a bafflement possibly legible on their blank upturned faces, as story has it that his succeeding sermons were written in a more useful, and down-to-earth manner, focusing more on the weather and crops than on biblical exegesis.

More than just a deliverer of sermons, Herbert acted as the doctor to the parish, with his wife his assistant and their garden his pharmacy. He is said to have loved music, walking twice a week to Salisbury Cathedral to listen to the choristers and ministering to his parishioners along the way.

Few poems are thought to have been written during Herbert's years at Bemerton. He did, however, write a book in which he outlined the ideal behaviour and lifestyle of the country parson, for that is what he had become. He called it *A Priest to the Temple*. "The Country Parson is exceeding exact in his Life, being holy, just, prudent, temperate, bold, grave in all his ways … ", lines that describe Herbert's final years with Jane and his extended family at Bemerton.

Throughout the winter of 1632, the tuberculosis that had plagued Herbert for much of his life returned, and he found his body becoming weaker and weaker. He was no longer able to attend to his parish, or preach to his parishioners. "God has broken into my study and taken off my chariot wheels, I have nothing worthy of God," he is said to have exclaimed in his final weeks.

His good friend Ferrar had committed himself to a life of spiritual isolation at Little Gidding, yet was anxious for news of Herbert so sent Edmund Duncan to Bemerton. This proved to be an auspicious decision, as it was Duncan to whom Herbert entrusted his manuscript, asking him to read it through "and then, if he can think it may turn to the advantage of any dejected poor soul, let it be made public; if not, let him burn it; for I and it are less than the least of God's mercies." This was in 1633. Ferrar, of course, was well aware of the worth of what had come into his hands. He certainly did not burn it, and later that year Herbert's poems, under the title of *The Temple*, were published in Cambridge.

2

The Country Parson and 'The Church-Porch'

"the least of God's mercies"

We cannot be sure that Herbert himself had given *The Temple* this title, nor that he had added its sub title *Sacred Poems and Private Ejaculations* (the OED definition of this last word, dated 1625, is "the hasty utterance of prayers, emotional exclamations, etc … ") However, elsewhere in the accompanying letter to Ferrar, Herbert told him that he would find in the poems "a picture of the many spiritual conflicts that have passed between God and my soul before I could subject mine to the will of Jesus, my Master." We would not be straying too far into speculation, therefore, were we to accept some of these "Private Ejaculations" as being autobiographical, and so there may be good reason to look first into his prose book *A Priest to the Temple* to learn something more of the man, his aims and his beliefs. Again this title is open to some doubt. One can see the obvious connection with the title of the poems, but as all but two of its thirty seven chapters begin with the words "The country parson … ", words which constitute its sub-title, this is how we propose to refer to it.

Nicholas Ferrar had clearly lost no time in having *The Temple* published, even though there were a number of objections to be overcome before it was granted a licence, but *The Country Parson* seems to have presented problems of a different nature as its first appearance was delayed until 1652, almost twenty years after Herbert's death, and then only in a miscellany entitled *Herbert's Remains* edited by his first biographer, Barnabas Oley. This was at the high point of Puritan rule in England and it is not difficult to imagine the shudders that would have been brought about by those terrible words *Priest* and *Temple* on its title page. By the time of its first *separate* publication, in 1671, the world had changed again. The civil war was over. Charles II was on the throne. The Anglican church had been re-established and people looked back to George Herbert's days as having been a Golden Age for the church. The Preface reminds those "not born before the troubles broke forth … what a Halcyonian Calm, a Blessed Time of Peace, this Church of England had for many years." Of course no age is ever *Golden* to those living through it, but it is not hard to see why it might have looked so to those reading Herbert's book half a century after it had been written.

Reading it today, we find ourselves wondering who it was written *for*. Scholars recognise it as belonging to the "character sketch", a genre which had gained some popularity in the early seventeenth century, the best known example in Herbert's own day being Joseph Hall's *Characters of Virtues and Vices* (1608). But in his Preface, *The Author to the Reader*, Herbert first tells us that he wrote it for himself, "that I may have a mark to aim at: which also I will set as high as I can", adding in a characteristic image, "since he shoots higher that threatens the moon than he that aims at a tree." But he also refers to "others", by which he means his fellow clergy. It was never intended for the General Reader. And Izaak Walton, in his biography of Herbert, recommends it as "A book so full of plain, prudent and useful rules that that country parson that can spare 12 pence and yet wants it (*does not have it*) is scarce excusable; because it will both direct him what he ought to do and convince (*make him feel guilty*) him for not having done it."

Walton, it has to be said, was guilty of not only idealising but idolising his man and giving rise to the "Holy George Herbert" image. This did him no favours. Herbert was not a saint. The aristocrat – sometimes quick-tempered, sometimes haughty – is still evident in the pages of *The Country Parson*, and it is a stronger and more honest book because of it. He was a realist. As he said at the start of Chapter 28, "The country parson knows well ... the general ignominy which is cast upon the profession (and that) he must be despised." Not long before this, Shakespeare had created the foolish cleric Sir Nathaniel in *Love's Labour Lost*. Fielding would soon be introducing Parson Adams to the world and Mr Collins is by no means Jane Austen's only stomach-turning vicar.

One of the "many spiritual conflicts" Herbert referred to in his letter to Ferrar was the question of his ordination. Was it a fit calling for a gentleman, and equally, was this particular gentlemen fit to answer such a calling?

A friend at court, on learning of his intentions, told him that it was "too mean an employment, and too much below his birth, and the excellent abilities and endowments of his mind." Herbert knew what he meant and accepted that "the iniquity of the late times have made ... the sacred name of Priest contemptible", but argued that he would "labour to make it honourable by consecrating all my learning and all my poor abilities to advance the glory of that God that gave them." This is the driving force behind much of *The Country Parson* and explains an unusual word Herbert uses in his opening chapter when he refers to a priest as Christ's *viceregent*. It is put to us as the highest of callings and very early he warns those who might be chaplains in great houses to remember their position and not to fall into "over-submissiveness and cringings."

The tone of high moral seriousness can be tedious, but is enlivened by the glimpses we are given into everyday seventeenth-century life, as when he tells the country parson what sorts of behaviour he ought not to tolerate in his church. Here Herbert is probably giving us a fairly accurate, and certainly a very vivid account of what often did go on. Reverence could be in rather short supply apparently and instead of attending to the service, the village people would often be talking to each other, gawping about or falling asleep. And when they were meant to kneel they would often just slouch or lean forward a bit. This had to be stopped. They were to attend "to what is done in the church, and everyone, man and child, answering aloud both Amen and all other answers, which are on the clerk's and people's part to answer; which answers are not to be done in huddling, or slubbering fashion, gaping and scratching the head, or spitting even in the midst of their answers, but gently and pauseable, thinking what they say."

And the gentry were seemingly no better. They would not deign to enter at the same time as the common people, but would wander in half-way through the service, making sure they were the centre of attention. It is such a Hogarthian picture that Herbert draws for us: none of your thatch and hollyhocks-round-the-door idealism of country life in these pages. Country people are "thick and heavy" he tells us, but this is something he seems to accept as a fact. It does not make him care for them any the less. The country parson should never disdain, "to enter into the poorest cottage, though he even creep into it and though it smell never so loathsomely."

On festival days, in contrast to the hovels they had come from, he ensures that the church is strewn with fresh rushes and perfumed with incense, however, one cannot but feel some sympathy for the peasantry, obliged to sit there every Sunday, knowing that each individual was being watched and that for any misdemeanour they would be severely spoken to. And spoken to they were in the service. "… the parson exceeds not an hour in preaching, because all ages have thought that a competency." At least if Herbert's advice were followed, attempts were made to see that the sermons were relevant to the experience of country people. Reminding his readers of Christ's parables, he puts it to them that, "the naming of a plough, a hatchet, a bushel of leaven can serve for lights even of heavenly truths."

Largely ignored by critics is Herbert's collection of over one thousand proverbs, published in 1640 under the title *Jacula Prudentum, or Outlandish Proverbs*. "*Outlandish*" in this context, probably meaning *foreign* rather than *unconventional* or *ridiculous* as many of them seem to have been translated from French, Italian and Spanish. They are examples of what might be called 'folk wisdom': *A good bargain is a pick-purse; Truth and oil are ever above*. Some are specifically Christian: *He loseth nothing that loseth not God.* And such sayings might well have played an important part in Herbert's sermons. As we will see, 'domestic' imagery is a marked feature of his lyrics.

One of his proverbs reads, *When God is made master of a family, he orders the disorderly,* and servants dwelling in the parson's household clearly lived under a very strict regime indeed. Chapter 10, 'The Parson in his House', begins, uncompromisingly, "The parson is very exact in the governing of his house", adding that "his family is a school of religion".

When we read Walton's *Life,* and certainly when we read the poems, there is nothing to suggest that there was anything of the kill-joy puritan about Herbert, yet the life-style he advocates does seem very austere. Every Friday is a day of abstinence, not only of diet, "but also of company, recreation and all outward contentments." And when it was a day of fasting, the diet was not only to be meagre but unpleasant. "For since fasting in Scripture language is an affecting of our souls, if a piece of dry flesh at my table be more unpleasant to me than the same fish there, certainly to eat the flesh, and not the fish, is to keep the fasting day naturally." This to him seemed *natural.*

It is difficult to equate the *gentle* George Herbert of tradition with the harshness of his attitude towards servants. "He keeps his servants between love and fear, according as he finds them; but generally he distributes it thus: to his children he shows more love than terror, to his servants more terror than love." There is really no way of softening that word *terror.* Perhaps he was more gentle in practice than in theory. Similarly, the description he gives of Prayer in the poem of that name: "Softness, and peace, and joy, and love, and bliss" seems very far removed from the rigid family discipline he advocates in this guide.

The country parson's care was meant to extend well beyond the bounds of his immediate family of course, and far beyond their spiritual needs.

He should, Herbert says, also be a lawyer and a physician, settling their disputes and tending to their ailments. And it is here, when he turns physician, that we are once again given one of those insights into seventeenth-century life and especially herbalism, "where the manifold wisdom of God is wonderfully to be seen." The herb garden will meet all needs and far more economically than the apothecary. "… elder, camomile, mallows, comfrey and smallage made into a poultice have done great and rare cures." And there is no need to buy costly spices when you have rosemary, thyme and mint growing outside your door.

And it was not only the poor he concerned himself with. The younger sons of the gentry were a particular problem. "The great and national sin of this land," he asserted, was idleness. We read of young men "spending the day in dressing, complimenting, visiting and sporting." On the question of *dressing,* perhaps he had forgotten his own undergraduate days, when Walton tells us, "his clothes seemed to prove that he put too great a value on his parts and parentage." Those days were over, but we can feel pretty sure that he had never ever said, "Come, we have nothing to do, let's go to the tavern, or to the stews (brothel) or what not." Or that he fell "to drink, to steal, to whore, to scoff, to revile, to all sorts of gamings."

Such young men would do better, he argues, to give their time to what today we would call service to the community, either by entering parliament, or becoming a Justice of the Peace, "an honourable employment of a gentle- or a nobleman in the country (*county*) he lives in, enabling him with power to do good and to restrain all those who might else trouble him and the whole state."

Reading this chapter (Chapter 30, 'The Parson's Consideration of Providence') it is interesting to remember Izaac Walton's frequent assertion that Herbert's acceptance of the living of Bemerton was a retreat from worldly ambitions to a simpler religious vocation. It makes for a good and saintly biography, but is it absolutely true? The previous incumbent, Dr Curle, had left to become Bishop of Bath and Wells and not long after that was promoted to the see of Winchester, so it was by no means a dead-end to preferment within the church and it is possible to look on *The Country Parson* as a way of Herbert advertising his abilities.

What makes us feel that Walton misjudged Herbert is a certain *authoritarian* tone we meet with throughout these pages. Herbert's love and concern for his lowly parishioners is never in any doubt, but then neither is the awareness of the social gulf between them and him. It is a fact of the times. As well as his love and concern, no single aspect of their lives escapes his *scrutiny*. He is in control and no one should ever doubt that. *The Country Parson* is perhaps more of a political document than is always recognised and could be said to be a programme for church government at a local level. We need to remind ourselves that it was written during the reign of Charles I and reflects that Stuart political ideal of centralisation and the imposition from the centre of obedience and conformity to the norms and practices of the Church of England. The aim would be the absolute control of the parishioners' spiritual, moral, political and material lives by a clergy who were a university-educated social élite – the watchdogs of the establishment.

Granted this seems like a far remove from the country parson of Walton's *Life*, "who died like a saint, unspotted of the world, full of alms deeds, full of humility, and all the examples of a virtuous life." But it is not to deny that picture. It adds a different aspect. Herbert, the parson, was still the man he had always been: the aristocrat and the politician. This is not to lessen his status. It makes him more complex, more human and far more interesting. It also helps us to understand that long, didactic poem 'The Church-Porch' which stands at the beginning of the collection, but which, from its title alone, is seen to stand outside the central core of the lyrics – *The Temple*.

Its seventy-seven stanzas are addressed to a "sweet youth", possibly his younger brother, Henry, who appears to be in need of moral guidance, and Herbert addresses him in verse in the belief that:

> A verse may find him, who a sermon flies,
> And turn delight into a sacrifice.
>
> (5-6)

Delight is in fairly short supply though in 'The Church-Porch'. It is for the most part a trawl through the Seven Deadly Sins and four of the Ten Commandments. For instance:

> Be thrifty, but not covetous: therefore give
> Thy need, thine honour, and thy friend his due.
> Never was scraper brave man. Get to live;
> Then live, and use it: else, it is not true
>   That thou hast gotten. Surely use alone
>   Makes money not a contemptible stone.
>
> (151-156)

It reminds us of Polonius, but without the laughs, and is very clumsy verse.

Proverbs held a fascination for Herbert; and it seems here that aphorism is what he is aiming at, but he is far too verbose. There is none of that precision and snap which made so many of Alexander Pope's epigrammatic lines *become* proverbs; "A little learning is a dangerous thing", for example, or "Fools rush in where angels fear to tread." Herbert's tread is far too heavy and the result can be verses which are both banal and pompous.

> Laugh not too much: the witty man laughs least:
> For wit is news only to ignorance .
> Less at thine own things laugh; lest in the jest
> Thy person share, and the conceit advance.
>   Make not thy sport, abuses: for the fly
>   That feeds on dung, is coloured thereby.
>
> (229-234)

Compared with the great lyrics which are to follow, what is most lacking is any awareness that there might possibly be some struggle or conflict involved in the avoidance of sin.

It is a poem which has never attracted much interest or support. One critic has described it as a large and worldly dragon before the portals of the church. Only W.H. Auden has spoken up for it. He included it in its entirety in his brief collection of Herbert's poems, adding, "One expects to be utterly bored, but thanks to Herbert's wit, one is entertained." Of course Auden was never more entertaining himself than when he was being cantankerous.

3

Metaphysical Poetry

"catching the sense at two removes"

The writing of literary criticism would be that much simpler if only we could draw up a neat timetable showing the changes which have taken place in all the varied schools and movements over the years, but sadly this can not be done. Reality is rarely, if ever, neat. *Metaphysical Poetry*, for instance – intellectual, assertive and dramatic – can be seen as a reaction against the mellifluous lyricism of the poetry of the Elizabethans. However, if we look closely at the way things were in the year 1593, the year of Herbert's birth, we find that the publication of Spenser's *The Faerie Queene*, written in praise of Elizabeth I, was still three years away. Shakespeare had not yet even written *Romeo and Juliet*, and it would be another sixteen years before the appearance of his *Sonnets*, yet John Donne, always thought of as a seventeenth-century poet, had already begun work on his own *Songs and Sonets*, which are regarded in the histories of English Literature as heralding the commencement of the 'Metaphysical School of Poetry'. Was he then reacting against poems which were still to be written?

It is not quite such a jumble, but the warning signs do have to be heeded. In the 1580s Sir Philip Sidney had written a sequence of love sonnets entitled *Astrophel and Stella* and their romantic delicacy and Petrarchan idealism were soon to be imitated in a flood of such sequences, Shakespeare's being only one among many and his appearing when the fashion was almost over. He did of course surpass his predecessors, but the opening lines of *Sonnet 76*:

> Why is my verse so barren of new pride?
> So far from variation or quick change?

suggest that even he felt his approach, his language and his imagery to be somewhat out of date. And if we put his most famous sonnet, "Shall I compare thee to a Summers day" alongside some stanzas from one of John Donne's love poems, 'A Valediction Forbidding Mourning', there is no doubt about it. Donne it is who has the 'variation and quick change'. He tells his lover not to weep for him when he goes away because their love is so much greater than that of ordinary people it quite surpasses the need for physical contact, or even physical presence.

> Moving of th'earth brings harmes and feares,
> Men reckon what it did and meant,
> But trepidation of the spheres,
> Though greater farre, is innocent.
>
> Dull sublunary lovers' love
> (Whose soul is sense) cannot admit
> Absence, because it doth remove
> Those things which elemented it.
>
> But we by a love, so much refin'd,
> That our selves know not what it is,
> Inter-assured of the mind,
> Care lesse, eyes, lips and hands to miss.
>
> (9-20)

Even to understand these verses is challenge enough. There is no gentle delicacy of feeling here, nor is there any delicacy of language. This is the language of the sciences: *trepidation, sublunary, elemented*. It is the language of the intellect and in the stanzas which follow, and which bring the poem to a close, we are presented with the language of mathematics and of logical reasoning.

> If they be two, they are two so
> As stiffe twin compasses are two,
> Thy soule the fixt foot, makes no show
> To move, but doth, if the other doe.
>
> And though it in the center sit
> Yet when the other far doth rome,
> It leanes and hearkens after it,
> And grows erect, as that comes home.
>
> Such wilt thou be to mee, who must
> Like th'other foot, obliquely runne;
> Thy firmness makes my circle just,
> And makes me end, where I begunne.
>
> (25-36)

Reasoning? Logical? Those small words which are so crucial to logical argument – *if, though* and *yet* – are certainly there, but surely the idea is totally *unreasonable*. There is no possible way in which the lovers' souls can be like "stiffe twin compasses". And yet, with wit and ingenuity, Donne *proves* that they are. And this is one of the poem's chief delights: its audacious and witty display of intellect. Yet there is no question that this *is* a love poem. The emotion is evident. What is different is that there is no separation here between the head and the heart. Logical argument and passionate feeling were not held to be mutually exclusive. As T.S. Eliot famously said of John Donne and his followers, they were " … men who incorporated their erudition into their sensibility."

It was this unusual display of erudition which earned such poets the label of 'metaphysical' and while critics have increasingly and rightly expressed their wish that the term had never come into use in the first place, it is too late now. Our passion for labels means that it persists and so still needs to be explained, or rather explained away.

And yet, while it began as a term of mockery, even of abuse, there is an element of truth in it. It is a term made up of two component parts. *Meta* is a Greek word which means *after*, but which later, and particularly in this context, came to mean *beyond*. So *metaphysics* is the philosophical study of that which is beyond the (*merely*) physical, i.e. abstract notions such as the essence of being, the nature of reality, and of things spiritual. The poets to whom this label has been attached – Donne, Herbert, Marvell and Crashaw – certainly did explore the realities of love and death, and what it means to have faith and to believe in God. But these are themes which had occupied poets long before and long since those early years of the seventeenth century. What made them different, and what earned them this dubious title, was the way in which they went about it – that tone which has already been described as *intellectual, assertive and dramatic*.

When it was first applied, the term does seem to have been one of mockery. John Dryden, in a contemptuous reference to the generation of poets before him (poets are always contemptuous of the generation before them) wrote of Donne, "He affects the metaphysics … in his amorous verses … and perplexes the minds of the fair sex with nice speculations of philosophy, where he should engage their hearts, and entertain them with the softnesses of love." Dryden was by no means as pompous or as patronising as this makes him sound, and his objections to what he saw as the eccentricities of early seventeenth-century verse are easy to understand. In their very excessiveness they were seen as an aspect of that political and religious ferment which had led to the abandonment of authority, the execution of the king and a bloody civil war. No one wanted a return to any of that – not in politics, not in religion and not in literature either. Complex verse forms, which had once been popular, gave way to the decorum, lucidity and regularity of the heroic couplet. Poetry became not a private, but a public medium for the expression of ideas and was, above all, to be rational. Imagination was to be reined in by judgement. As the critic Thomas Rhymer put it in 1678, "A poet is not to leave his reason and blindly abandon himself to follow fancy, for then his fancy might be monstrous, might be singular, and please nobody's maggot but his own; but reason is to be his guide, reason is common to all people, and can never carry him from what is Natural."

Dryden singled out George Herbert for particular mockery. Herbert occasionally enjoyed such 'unnatural' things, such instances of 'false wit', as acrostics, anagrams, and poems the likes of his 'Easter-Wings' and 'The Altar', where the *shape* of the poem on the page replicates that of the actual subject. In one of his satires Dryden dismissed a rival poet as only fit to:

> command
> Some peaceful Province in Acrostic land,
> There mayst thou Wings display and Altars raise,
> And torture one poor Word a Thousand Ways.

> (*Mac Flecknoe*, 206-208)

These were things too trivial to be worth serious note and after 1709 there was not a single edition of Herbert's poems published for another ninety years, during which time Samuel Johnson, the eighteenth century's most influential critic, coined the term 'metaphysical poets' and drove some definitive nails into their coffin. Interestingly, neither Donne nor Herbert was included in his *Lives of the Poets*; it was Abraham Cowley he chose to write about, and at length. To us this looks decidedly odd, as Cowley is a forgotten figure. In his own day however he had been rated very highly indeed, but if we do read him at all now it strikes us that those 'metaphysical' features which had seemed to come so naturally to Donne, appear in Cowley like affectations, effects he had had to strive hard for. There is a good deal of verbal ingenuity, but it is superficial; there is no real depth of thought or feeling there. But Johnson's objections were not confined to Cowley; they included all the 'authors of this race'. He damns them all by claiming that, "Their wish was only to say what they hoped had never been said before." And how did they manage that? "The most heterogeneous ideas are yoked by violence together; nature and art are ransacked for illustrations, comparisons, and allusions." And "thoughts so far-fetched, as to be not only unexpected, but unnatural". They are guilty, says

Johnson, of "enormous and disgusting hyperboles", fictions "violent and unnatural", or else "slight and trifling". All in all "their thoughts and expressions" were "grossly absurd". The only concession he seemed prepared to make was that "To write on this plan, it was at least necessary to read and think". It is hardly surprising that after a condemnation on that scale, John Donne and his followers should have fallen from favour.

Readers in the eighteenth century seem to have concentrated their attention on the imagery. What they failed to appreciate was the dramatic vitality of these poems. Writing his 'Elegie upon the death of the Dean of Pauls, Dr John Donne' in 1631, Thomas Carew makes a clear reference to Donne's sweeping away of the Petrarchan clichés of Elizabethan love lyrics:

> The Muses garden with Pedantique weedes
> O'rspread, was purg'd by thee; The lazie seeds
> Of servile imitation throwne away,
> And fresh invention planted.

But, and more significantly, he later refers to Donne's "line of masculine expression".

Two distinct types of literature were dominant in Elizabethan England: the lyric and the drama. Donne was, we have been told, "a great frequenter of plays" and it was his appropriation of the virile language of the drama for his love lyrics which led to one of the most audacious rebellions in the whole of English literature. There had never before been love poems which began with outbursts such as:

> Busie old foole, unruly Sunne,
> Why dost thou thus,
> Through windowes and through curtaines call on us?

('The Sunne Rising')

or:

> For Godsake hold your tongue, and let me love,

('The Cannonization')

He even adopted the same tone in his religious verse:

> Batter my heart, three-person'd God;

('Holy Sonnet')

His were not the usual gentle meditations on the pains of unrequited love. This love was requited and in the most explicitly sexual way.

> Licence my roving hands, and let them go,
> Behind, before, above, between, below.
> O my America! my new-found land.

> ('Elegie: Going to Bed')

It is the speaking voice one is most aware of. These poems could be read as dramatic soliloquies. At other times one is conscious of a second person – even though silent – being an essential part of the scene, as in Donne's 'The Flea', or Andrew Marvell's 'To His Coy Mistress'.

> Had we but World enough, and Time,
> This coyness, Lady, were no crime.
> We would sit down, and think which way
> To walk, and pass our long Loves day.

> ('To His Coy Mistress')

George Herbert wrote no love poems. His themes are exclusively religious, but he nevertheless learned from Donne's example. There are the same dramatic beginnings:

> I struck the board, and cried, No more,
>   I will abroad.
> What? shall I ever sigh and pine?

> ('The Collar')

And the same conversations with others, notably with God Himself.

> My God, I heard this day,
> That none doth build a stately habitation,
>   But that he means to dwell therein.

> ('Man')

Herbert's imagery is every bit as unexpected and as vivid as Donne's. His craftsmanship is unparalleled and his explorations of religious experience have a depth which only Gerard Manley Hopkins has ever approached.

In his *Biographia Literaria* Coleridge extended a gentle nod of approval in Herbert's direction. He praised the "simple dignity of the language", but at a later date he did much to encourage the belief that it was impossible to appreciate his verse unless one was "likewise a *Christian*, and both a zealous and an orthodox, both a devout and a *devotional* Christian". There were many editions of Herbert during the nineteenth century, but he continued to be appreciated for his piety rather than his poetry. Serious critical attention was reserved for the Romantics and for Tennyson and Browning. It was not until 1921 and Grierson's acclaimed anthology *Metaphysical Lyrics & Poems of the Seventeenth Century: Donne to Butler* that the blinkers finally fell off. The time was right, for the times coincided. The 1920s were a decade of great unrest. Britain was still trying to recover from a devastating war. The rise of the Labour movement was changing the social scene and beginning to overturn the traditional political power base. Old values, Edwardian values, no longer seemed relevant. Women, who had played a major role in the war effort, were campaigning for greater rights. And 1921 was also the year in which Einstein won the Nobel Prize for Physics. Two hundred years before, the Civil War had been the cause of similar social, political and religious unrest. Science was then changing the way people understood their world and voyages of discovery had brought to light new worlds. These were times which spoke to each other. And so, not surprisingly, a similar revolution took place in the poetry. Just as Donne and his contemporaries had rejected the gentle lyricisms of a previous age, so the Georgians (equally pastoral and lyrical) were cast aside and the new poetry, that of T.S. Eliot and Ezra Pound, was of a kind which also provided a demanding intellectual challenge.

While Grierson's anthology re-established John Donne as a leading literary figure, Herbert remained in his shadow for many years. Donne's influence on Herbert is there to be seen and is hardly surprising. Twenty-one years his senior, Donne's reputation was such that he was already preaching to vast open-air crowds at Paul's Cross when Herbert was being awarded his MA. Moreover, Donne was not a remote figure; he was a close family friend and someone the young Herbert would no doubt have looked up to and admired. It was to Herbert's mother, Magdalen, he addressed that gentle and moving tribute 'The Autumnall' which begins:

> No Spring nor Summer Beauty hath such grace
> As I have seen in an Autumnall face

And when she died in 1627 it was John Donne who preached her funeral sermon. There can be little doubt, therefore, that while Donne's poems were not published until the year of Herbert's death, he had read them as a young man when they were being circulated in manuscript among the poet's friends.

The differences between these two poets are, however, distinct and significant. Herbert, unlike Donne, not only wrote no love poems, he wrote no poems at all of a secular nature. In a letter written to his mother when he was still in his teens he declared his "resolution to be, that my poor abilities in poetry shall be all, and ever consecrated to God's glory." And it was a resolution from which he never wavered.

The differences between Donne and Herbert could be thought of as being reflected (but not occasioned) by their different positions in the Church. The voluptuousness of Donne matches the grandeur of St Paul's where he was Dean, whereas Herbert's tiny parish of Bemerton befits his greater simplicity. But we must not overemphasise that simplicity or we end up with Walton's "saintly poet". Herbert was more aristocratic than Donne. He could be vain, haughty and quick-tempered. He had been Public Orator at Cambridge University and while we do not, as we do with Donne, have his published sermons to read, he might well have been his equal in that ability when he chose. There are certainly more voices to be heard in Herbert than in Donne.

4

The 'Hieroglyphic Poems'

"*in acrostic land*"

Writing in his *Memoir* in the latter half of the eighteenth century, William Cowper tells us how he met with Herbert's poems during one of his fits of depression, "and gothic and uncouth as they are, yet I found in them a strain of piety, which I could not but admire." And not many years later, Coleridge wrote, "I find more substantial comfort now in pious George Herbert's *Temple*, which I used to read to amuse myself with his quaintness, in short only to laugh at." Clearly, it was the piety rather than the poetry which kept Herbert's name alive. The poetry was looked upon as *gothic, uncouth* and *quaint*. All so very old-fashioned. And in this we are reminded of Dryden's dismissive and sarcastic remark about "Some peaceful Province in Acrostic land". It is true that verbal games – anagrams, acrostics and suchlike – had been more fashionable in Elizabethan times. In the first act of *Romeo and Juliet*, we remember, the lovers' exchange during the dance is in fact a regular sonnet. Artificial, but delightful.

In Herbert's hands, these displays of wit are far more than simply games. In 'The Forerunners', a brilliant poem in which, nevertheless, he laments that he seems to have lost the ability to write poems, he says that at least he can still write '*Thou art still my God*', and God will be pleased with that.

> He will be pleased with that ditty;
> And if I please him, I write fine and witty.
>
> (11-12)

So even a plain statement can be *witty*.

Wit is one of those weasel words one has to approach with great care. In this context it has nothing to do with repartee or jokes. It comes from the German verb *wissen* – to know – from which we also derive *wise* and *wisdom*, and so, for Herbert, it meant intelligence, and, where poetry was concerned, it also meant imagination. For a poem to be *witty* it needed to have a degree of intellectual glamour about it, some urbanity and daring.

It might indeed be funny. It might certainly occasion some *mirth*, but again that is a word to be cautious about. When Herbert remarked that "Religion does not banish mirth, but only moderates it and sets rules to it", he was not thinking of frivolity. Frivolity cannot be set rules. In artistic terms, *mirth* could mean something close to *embellishment*, a quality which could be moderated, but to judge from Herbert's use of the word in his verse, for example, in 'The Dawning', "Thy Saviour comes and with him mirth", it would seem to be an emotion – one of religious joy, and associated with redemption and grace.

Looking back at 'The Forerunners' we read "My God must have my best", and this certainly included *wit*. The intelligence and the word-play Herbert would have demonstrated when Public Orator at Cambridge were not pushed to one side when he came to write poems, but a closer look at some of the poems of that nature, and which have at times been labelled 'hieroglyphic', will show that they are by no means all surface glitter.

What Dryden had singled out for particular scorn in *Acrostic Land* were poems in the shape of *Wings* and *Altars*, and Herbert of course was 'guilty' on both counts.

The Altar

<pre>
        A   broken   ALTAR,   Lord,   thy   servant   rears,
      Made   of   a   heart,   and   cemented   with   tears:
            Whose parts are as thy hand did frame;
            No workman's tool hath touched the same.
                        A   HEART   alone
                        Is   such   a   stone,
                        As   nothing   but
                        Thy pow'r doth cut.
                        Wherefore each part
                        Of   my   hard   heart
                        Meets in this frame,
                        To praise thy name:
            That if I chance to hold my peace,
            These stones to praise thee may not cease.
      O   let   thy   blessed   SACRIFICE   be   mine,
      And   sanctify   this   ALTAR   to   be   thine.
</pre>

Shape poems have in fact a long history to them, going back at least as early as the first century BC and the *Greek Anthology*, which featured one pair of wings

33

and two altars. But for Herbert to have used the word *altar* can be made to look somewhat controversial, as indeed can the title of his collection *The Temple*, with its contentious echoes of the kind of high-church splendour favoured by Archbishop Laud, and which was anathema to the growing band of puritans within the Church of England. But the word has other connotations. For instance, in a letter to his mother, Herbert described a true believer as being "a sacred Temple for God himself to dwell in", words which in themselves echo St. Paul's in 1 Corinthians 3:16 "Know ye not that ye are the temple of God, and that the spirit of God dwelleth in you." And similarly, there are two different ways of looking at *altar*. It is true that when communion tables were replaced by stone altars in the 1620s it was a deliberate and controversial act of defiance by those members of the catholic wing of the Anglican church who were in favour of a greater degree of ceremony, but Herbert's choice of the word was determined not so much by ideology as by poetic expediency, for, whereas for Christians the altar is where the Eucharist is celebrated, for the Israelites of Old Testament times it was where sacrifices were offered up. The poem depends on, and develops this contrast, putting forward the Christian belief that a contrite (i.e. *broken*) heart is the only fit and proper sacrificial offering.

Truly remarkable, as Chana Bloch has shown in her book *Spelling the Word*, is the number of direct and indirect references to the Bible that are to be found in this poem. Line four says of this altar that "No workman's tool hath touched the same", and Herbert may have confidently expected his readers to remember God's command in Deuteronomy 27: 5,6 "And there shalt thou build an altar unto the Lord thy God, an altar of stones: thou shalt not lift up any iron tool upon them." (Exodus 20:25 explains, "for if thou lift up thy tool upon it, thou hast polluted it.") And Deuteronomy continues " ... and thou shalt offer burnt offerings thereon unto the Lord thy God."

Now none of this would be fitting in a Christian church, of course, and even the Psalmist had recognised that "thou delightest not in burnt offering. The sacrifices of God are a broken spirit: a broken and contrite heart, O God, thou wilt not despise." (Psalm 51: 16,17) And so here, the altar is not only the speaker's heart, broken by suffering, it is also where Christ's body is broken in the Eucharist.

Man's hard heart, which only the grace of God can reach, is likewise reminiscent of Ezekiel 11:19 " ... and I will take the stony heart out of their flesh, and will give them an heart of flesh."

The sacrifice which God expects from the contrite heart is praise and thanksgiving – "To praise thy name" (l.12) and when the Communion Service is over and Christ's sacrifice has been celebrated on the altar, among the closing words of the congregation are " ... accept this our sacrifice of praise and thanksgiving." Herbert's praise and thanksgiving are there in his poems, but in lines 13/14 he seems to be saying that were he to stop writing, his heart would still cry out, and his words echo Christ on the Mount of Olives saying of his Apostles, "I tell you that if these should hold their peace, the stones would immediately cry out!" (Luke 19:40). Added to which are St. Paul's words about epistles, "written not with ink, but with the spirit of the living God; not in tables of stone, but in the fleshy tables of the heart." (2 Corinthians 3:3)

This extensive use which Herbert makes of the Bible is not, of course, limited to this particular poem. As Chana Bloch has shown, it is there throughout his work.

'The Altar' is followed appropriately by a poem entitled 'The Sacrifice' – spoken by the crucified Christ – and this has led scholars to speculate on the possibility that there is an overall shape and design to *The Temple*. There have been several suggestions and theories: a *chronological* arrangement, leading from Holy Week through the Christian Year back through Lent; a *theological* arrangement, leading from sin to salvation ; or a *spiritual* arrangement in which the soul grows in understanding of God's love through trials and discouragements to the quiet surrender of the final poem, 'Love III'. An *architectural* arrangement has been suggested, but the altar, while it may be the chief feature of a church, is not the first thing to meet the eye as you enter. The reality is probably that at some late stage of his life, Herbert, like any other poet, would have spread his work over the dining room table and said, 'Yes, these go together. And so do these.' There are certainly sequences within *The Temple*, but, as we see it, no overall design.

Herbert's other 'notorious' poem is 'Easter-Wings'.

> Lord, who createdst man in wealth and store,
> Though foolishly he lost the same,
> Decaying more and more,
> Till he became
> Most poor:
> With thee
> O let me rise
> As larks harmoniously,
> And sing this day thy victories:
> Then shall the fall further the flight in me.

My tender age in sorrow did begin:
And still with sicknesses and shame
Thou didst so punish sin,
That I became
Most thin.
With thee
Let me combine,
And feel this day thy victory:
For, if I imp my wing on thine,
Affliction shall advance the flight in me.

(Ideally these lines should be printed vertically on the page, as they were in the first edition of *The Temple*, so that they look more like wings.)

What we have here is not one pair of wings, but two pairs, as we learn from some verses in the Book of Kings, "And within the oracle he made two cherubims of olive tree, each ten cubits high. And five cubits was the one wing of the cherub, and five cubits the other wing of the cherub: from the uttermost part of the one wing unto the uttermost part of the other was ten cubits." (1 Kings 6:23,24) And the lines reflect this exactly: each 'wing' being of ten lines, made up of 2 x 5.

Addison was wrong to condemn this as an example of false wit, as it is far more than a piece of technical bravura. The poem has a clear sense of purpose: the exposition of the doctrine of 'The Fortunate Fall'. This is the belief that if Adam had *not* been expelled from Eden, God would not have needed to send his Son down to earth to die for us. Hence there would have been no Incarnation and no Redemption, in fact no Christianity, therefore the *Fall*, viewed from this perspective, was a *Fortunate* event.

The fullness of the opening line reflects the fullness of Eden with its "wealth and store", but then, because of man's folly, all this is lost, and the lines, following this decay, narrow and dwindle to the central point of the stanza as "most poor". But this is Easter and the celebration of the Resurrection, and so the poem opens out again as Herbert asks, "With thee/O let me rise". That he asks to rise like a *lark* has its significance too as the Latin for a lark is *alauda*, and contains the verb to *laud*, to *praise*. In the concluding line the reference to the *Fall* is explicit.

This first stanza began with what one might call a generalised statement, but the second is clearly more personal, calling to mind what we know of Herbert's own ill health, "Most thin". The shape of the stanza here suggests an hour-glass as well as wings. The passage of time is indicated not only by the falling motion, but by the verbs being in the past tense. Again, there follows a look towards the future. The tense changes and the words open out in flight. To *imp* is a term from falconry and is to graft feathers onto the wing of a damaged bird. Herbert is damaged by his sin, but if he can join with the risen Christ, sharing in his suffering he will share in His victory on this Easter Day, "Affliction shall advance the flight in me". *Affliction* is a particularly charged word for Herbert, for, as we shall see, he wrote five extremely personal poems with that same title. Another Bible echo of some significance here is from Malachi 4:2 "But unto you that fear my name shall the Son of Righteousness arise with healing in his wings." Recalling what Herbert had said in 'The Church-Porch', "A verse may find him who a sermon flies", there could be no more vivid way of giving voice to the doctrine of the Fall and though Addison and others might have scoffed at it, it is a poem which, once read, is never forgotten.

Inevitably, anagrams also tended to be looked down upon as examples of false wit and Herbert's

Ana-(Mary) gram
(Army)

How well her name an army doth present,
In whom the *Lord of Hosts* doth pitch his tent.

at first glance tempts one to say *Mary/Army*, yes, neat but rather obvious. *Obvious*, however, is just what George Herbert is not, and this seemingly straightforward anagram is a complex statement about the Incarnation.

The title splits the word *Anagram* into two. On one side is Ana, the name of Mary's mother, then comes Mary, then the Greek for *Word*. The sequence is there to be read – the sequence we are given in John 1:14 "And the Word was made flesh and dwelt among us". John's Gospel was written in Greek and the word which is translated here as *dwelt* is *eskenosen*, a word whose literal meaning is 'to pitch a tent', which explains the otherwise puzzling second line of the couplet.

The change of *Mary* into *Army* would have been far more meaningful to readers in Herbert's day, familiar with their Bibles, as in the Song of Solomon 6:10, "Who is she ... terrible as an army with banners" had long been accepted as an allegorical reference to the Virgin Mary.

Host is derived from the Latin for an *army* and the term *Lord of the Hosts* is a term we meet with in the Psalms. "The Lord of Hosts is with us" 46:11. The word *host* also suggests the bread of the Eucharist and *tent* can mean the tabernacle where the host is kept.

The thought process which went into the creation of such seemingly-simple complexity is hard to imagine, but it is not a case of meanings being read *into* the text; they are there waiting to be read.

In the memorial Window of St. Andrew's church in Bemerton, Herbert is shown holding his lute, and as Walton tells us, "His chiefest recreation was music, in which heavenly art he was a most excellent master." During the years he lived in Bemerton he would walk twice a week the few miles into Salisbury, where, he said, the "Cathedral music elevated his soul," and before walking home again "he would usually sing and play his part at an appointed private music evening." Music very often provides the imagery for his poems and sometimes even the structure, as in 'Sin's Round'.

Sin's Round

Sorry I am, my God, sorry I am,
That my offences course it in a ring,
My thoughts are working like a busy flame,
Until their cockatrice they hatch and bring:
And when they once have perfected their draughts,
My words take fire from my inflamèd thoughts.

My words take fire from my inflamèd thoughts,
Which spit it forth like the Sicilian hill.
They vent the wares, and pass them with their faults,
And by their breathing ventilate the ill.
But words suffice not, where are lewd intentions:
My hands do join to finish the inventions.

My hands do join to finish the inventions:
And so my sins ascend three stories high,
As Babel grew, before there were dissensions.
Yet ill deeds loiter not: for they supply
New thoughts of sinning: wherefore, to my shame,
Sorry I am, my God, sorry I am.

A *round* is both a country dance in which those taking part hold hands in a circle, and it is also a song in which the words are repeated over and again. Here the structure is such that the closing lines of stanzas one and two are repeated as the opening lines of stanzas two and three, while the final line of three repeats the first line of stanza one, so that it is a ring, or *round*. This can be taken as Herbert saying that there appears to be no end to his sinning and, as the congregation declares in the General Confession in the Book of

Common Prayer, he has sinned in *thought* (stanza one), *word* (stanza two), and *deed* (stanza three).

In the first stanza the imagery is that of fire and his thoughts are so "inflamèd" that they give birth to a cockatrice – a legendary creature shaped like a giant, winged rooster with the tail of a lizard. It could kill with one glance, but it was also associated with sin and in Isaiah 59:4-5 we read, " … they conceive mischief, and bring forth iniquity. They hatch cockatrice's eggs." Here again we have an example of just how much learning can lie behind Herbert's imagery, as in contemporary alchemy the cockatrice was a symbol of fire and often depicted with its tail in its mouth, thus completing a circle just as this poem itself does. Equally in line five, the word *draughts* can mean both the plans that are hatched and the air admitted to a furnace through the *draught-hole*.

Stanza two takes up the final line of stanza one, "My words take fire from my inflamèd thoughts" and the thoughts are followed by *words*, which, continuing the fire image, are spat out like larva from Mount Etna. Words are followed by evil deeds and his three sins are now "three stories high" and, like the Tower of Babel (Genesis 11:1-9), are an assault on heaven itself. Evil deeds are not slow in prompting "New thoughts of sinning" and so we are back where we began, except that we are at least offering up our penitence.

'A Wreath' is another poem where the structure is an integral part of the content: not a circle this time, but an intricate twisting and weaving. The first stanza reads:

> A wreathed garland of deserved praise,
> Of praise deserved, unto thee I give,
> I give to thee, who knowest all my ways,
> My crooked, winding ways, wherein I live,

And while this is the kind of complex action which would be required to wreathe a garland – a garland of praise – we quickly notice a problem. Herbert's ways, he admits, are "crooked winding ways" and in Proverbs 2:13-15 those "who leave the paths of righteousness [their] ways are crooked". Whereas the Psalmist (Psalm 5:8) prays "make thy ways straight before my face".

"Give me simplicity," Herbert asks in line nine, which seems oddly ironic in a poem of such complexity and which began by offering God "A wreathed garland". Herbert may possibly have confused himself here.

But just how much and varied meaning he was able to pack into a very little space is best demonstrated by 'Trinity Sunday', a poem which celebrates the Trinity in a poem of three stanzas, each of three lines and employing only three rhymes.

Trinity Sunday

Lord, who hast formed me out of mud,
    And hast redeemed me through thy blood ,
    And sanctified me to do good;

Purge all my sins done heretofore;
    For I confess my heavy score,
    And I will strive to sin no more.

Enrich my heart, mouth, hands in me,
    With faith, with hope, with charity;
    That I may run, rise, rest with thee.

In the triplet in stanza one man is formed, redeemed and sanctified. In stanza two we read of his state of sin in the past, the present and the future. We then come to the brilliance of stanza three which in its first line looks again at the sins of *thought, word* and *deed,* but in the second line they are 'enriched' by the three primary virtues *faith, hope* and *charity.* Faith stems from the heart. Hope is expressed through the mouth and deeds of charity are performed with the hands. These will enable him, in a third and alliterative triplet to "run, rise and rest with thee", verbs which call to mind directly three crucial texts from the New Testament. (Hebrews 12:1) "Let us run with patience the race that is set before us". (1 Thessalonians 4:10) "The dead in Christ shall rise", and (Matthew 11:28) "I will give you rest".

Few, I think, would question, however, that Herbert's most complex poem is 'Prayer I' – the sonnet without a main verb.

Prayer I

Prayer, the Church's banquet, Angels' age,
    God's breath in man returning to his birth,
    The soul in paraphrase, heart in pilgrimage,
The Christian plummet sounding heav'n and earth;
Engine against th'Almighty, sinners' tower,
    Reversed thunder, Christ-side-piercing spear,
    The six-days world-transposing in an hour,
A kind of tune, which all things hear and fear;
Softness, and peace, and joy, and love, and bliss,
    Exalted Manna, gladness of the best,

> Heaven in ordinary, man well dressed,
>> The milky way, the bird of Paradise,
>>> Church-bells beyond the stars heard, the soul's blood,
>>> The land of spices, something understood.

To suggest, as it has been, that this poem fails ultimately because it does not define prayer is surely to misunderstand both the poem and prayer. To define is to establish the limits of something, and what Herbert is telling us here is that there are no limits to prayer. *Angels' age* is eternity (Luke 20:36).

The most important thing this poem has to say about prayers – be they formal or informal – is that they are not simply a one-sided recitation of words. Prayer entails a relationship with God and is reciprocal. This is evident from line two, where the image is taken from Genesis 2, "And the Lord God formed man ... and breathed into his nostrils the breath of life." This breathing-in, this inspiration, is what we return to God, Herbert is saying, when we pray. Similarly, the "Exalted Manna" of line ten is the returning to God of the blessing of the manna which he gave to the Israelites. Manna is "the bread which the Lord hath given you to eat," said Moses, (Exodus 16:15) and being "Exalted"; suggests the elevation of the host during the Mass. A prayer is an offering to God in exchange for what he has given us.

The variety of images here is telling us that there are many different ways of praying. In the second quatrain there is a change: a new violence. An *Engine* is an instrument of war and (Jove's) thunder is being hurled back at the heavens. It is a violence which reminds us that our prayers are sometimes occasioned by our anger at what seems to us to be unjust – outbursts of rage and rebellion. Such moods of rebellion can be quite explicit in Herbert's poems, for example 'The Collar' (which may also be pronounced *choler)* which begins, "I struck the board, and cried, No more". In contrast to this violence, the final six lines, relaxed and sensuous, feel like moments filled with divine grace.

To 'explain' any more of the twenty-six images for prayer in this poem might be to damage it, as they are meant to invoke an individual response and if we pause to consider each separate one they become clear enough. The problem, if it is a problem, comes when we try to consider the poem as a whole. Its outer structure is that of a regular sonnet (though the rhymes of lines 9-12 are slightly irregular) but within this firm structure all is a restless swirl of images, a veritable kaleidoscope of words which will not keep still. As we read we feel forever on the verge of grasping it, and then just as we know that we really haven't, Herbert tells us that it is "something understood". It is an ending which leaves us silent, knowing that it is a poem which we will never quite have finished reading.

The seven poems we have looked closely at in this chapter – varied in form though they are – tell us one thing very clearly: that George Herbert enjoyed writing poetry. The enjoyment is there in the challenges which he set himself. He rises to the challenge of difficulty, and, as he declared in a poem entitled 'The Son', and which is self-evidently true, "I like our language".

5

Poems on Poetry

"I like our language"

The opening lines of 'The Son' read:

> Let foreign nations of their language boast,
> What fine variety each tongue affords:
> I like our language, as our men and coast:
> Who cannot dress it well, want wit, not words.

As we have just seen, George Herbert did not *want* (i.e. *lack*) wit, and the English language at that time was certainly something the country could boast of. In terms of vocabulary alone, it was expanding in a totally unprecedented way, and not only because of the work of the great Renaissance classical scholars; discoveries in science, technology and travel were adding new words all the time. It was also an age blessed with writers of immense literary skill and invention – Jonson, Marlowe, Shakespeare, and that extraordinarily gifted group of men who gave us the King James Bible.

Herbert, we also need to remember, had been brought up by one of the most remarkable of women, in a household where intellect was valued, where John Donne – who excelled not only in poetry, but in prose and oratory too – was a frequent visitor. And we should not overlook the literary abilities of that dashing elder brother of his, Edward, a philosopher of some daring and originality and a metaphysical poet in his own right. From his earliest years, George Herbert was accustomed to hearing language being *used*, and used eloquently. And as he grew older, his own education at Westminster School and Trinity College, could hardly have been bettered. "I know the ways of learning," he wrote at the beginning of 'The Pearl', and that was no idle boast. Yet, in all his poems, he wore his learning lightly, and despite the extent of his reading in Greek and Latin, classical allusions are conspicuous by their total absence. Instead, the literary source he relied on was the Bible, and for the most part his language, as in Christ's parables, was of the simplest and homeliest. As he put it in *The Country Parson* "This is the skill, and doubtless the Holy Scripture intends thus much when it condescends to the naming of a plough, a hatchet, a bushel of leaven, boys piping and dancing; showing that things of ordinary use are not only to serve in the way of drudgery, but to be washed and cleansed, and serve for lights even of heavenly truths."

In 'Affliction I' he says of his feelings of inadequacy and uselessness "a blunted knife was of more use than I", an image as surprising, and as exact, as any of the intellectual extravagancies of his contemporaries. And in the same poem he writes of his hopes for the future:

> Now I am here, what thou wilt do with me
> > None of my books will show:
> I read, and sigh, and wish I were a tree;
> > For sure then I should grow
> To fruit or shade: at least some bird would trust
> Her household to me, and I should be just.
>
> > > > (55-60)

Such images from nature play an important part in Herbert's work, and they are not simply traditional, hand-me-down things, but are based on what he himself had seen, as we can tell from a stanza in 'Man's Medley':

> > Not, that he may not here,
> > > Taste of the cheer,
> > But as birds drink, and straight lift up their head,
> > > So must he sip and think
> > > > Of better drink
> > He may attain to, after he is dead.
>
> > > > (19-24)

Before going further, it might be appropriate to point out the unusual stanza forms of these last two quotations – Herbert's own invention, each one, and never to be repeated by him. His technical skill is almost without parallel in this respect.

Flowers, too, feature widely in Herbert's poems, and not simply as decoration, but an essential part of the thought process, as emblem in fact, as in the poem 'Life':

I made a posy, while the day ran by;
Here will I smell my remnant out, and tie
                      My life within this band.
But time did beckon to the flowers, and they
By noon most cunningly did steal away,
                      And withered in my hand.

My hand was next to them, and then my heart:
I took, without more thinking, in good part
                      Time's gentle admonition:
Who did so sweetly death's sad taste convey,
Making my mind to smell my fatal day;
                      Yet sug'ring the suspicion.

Farewell dear flowers, sweetly your time ye spent,
Fit, while ye lived, for smell or ornament,
                      And after death for cures.
I follow straight without complaint or grief,
Since if my scent be good, I care not, if
                      It be as short as yours.

The emblem, or central metaphor here, for the brevity of human life comes from Psalm 103:15 " … the days of man are but as grass, for he flourisheth as a flower of the field.' His own days are like flowers, Herbert says, and he has gathered those which have passed so far into a posy – a word which, appropriately, can also mean a short poem. In line three he ties his life to them, but their time is so short that by noon they have died and withered in his hand. At this point we realise that this poem, although called 'Life' is about death, seen here as Time. But this portrayal of time is not the threatening, cloaked figure with a scythe; he "did beckon" only to the flowers and though making the speaker aware of his own "fatal day", he does it while "sug'ring the suspicion".

In the third stanza Herbert separates himself from the flowers, bidding farewell to them, yet the analogy remains. Death is not a complete finality for them – dried they become medicinal "cures" and Herbert's seventeenth-century spelling allows him to end on the image of him being *sent* to God.

Classical poets, including of course Herrick, would have used the passing of flowers and the brevity of human life as a motif for a *carpe diem* theme: "Gather ye rosebuds while ye may". But in Herbert there is instead a quiet acceptance. "I care not," he concludes. It is evidence of a mind greatly at peace with itself and with its beliefs.

For all that it might be accused of a certain naivety, there is a quiet magnificence to this poem, and as the American scholar, Arnold Stein, putting the point more academically, says, it shows in Herbert "a highly developed intellectual power of imagining things in their absolute simplicity."

It is, however, what might be called 'domestic' simplicity which is recognised as Herbert's own and most telling hallmark. In 'Man', a poem detailing the many gifts which God has bestowed on us, we read:

> Nothing we see, but means our good,
> As our *delight*, or as our *treasure*:
> The whole is, either our cupboard of *food*,
> Or cabinet of *pleasure*.
>
> The stars have us to bed;
> Night draws the curtain, which the sun withdraws;
>
> (27-32)

And in 'Providence' there is an image, based on Christ's calming of the waters (Matthew 8:26) which few other poets would have dared, or could have carried off if they had.

> Tempests are calm to thee, they know thy hand,
> And hold it fast, as children do their father's,
> Which cry and follow.
>
> (45-47)

Helen Vendler may have been slightly overstating her case when she suggested that "few have attempted to judge Herbert as an artist, rather than as a guide for the Anglican perplexed", but there is some truth in what she says. "I like our language," he wrote. He enjoyed writing and it is not always recognised how many of his poems have the writing of poetry as their central topic.

In his *Life of Herbert* Isaak Walton quotes part of a letter sent to his mother, along with two sonnets, as a New Year's gift in 1610, his first year at university, when he was still only seventeen. In it he wrote that his aim was "to reprove the vanity of these many love-poems that are daily writ and consecrated to Venus." Love-poems? Could he perhaps have been thinking of Shakespeare? His 'sugar'd sonnets' had been published only the year before. He then went on to declare his "resolution to be, that my poor abilities in poetry shall be all, and ever consecrated to God's glory." The sonnets were to be 'testimony' to that resolution.

Sonnet I

My God, where is that ancient heat towards thee,
    Wherewith whole shoals of Martyrs once did burn,
    Besides their other flames? Doth poetry
Wear Venus' livery? only serve her turn?
Why are not sonnets made of thee? and lays
    Upon thine altar burnt? Cannot thy love
    Heighten a spirit to sound out thy praise
As well as any she? Cannot thy dove
Outstrip their Cupid easily in flight?
    Or, since thy ways are deep, and still the same,
    Will not a verse run smooth that bears thy name!
Why doth that fire, which by thy power and might
    Each breast doth feel, no braver fuel choose
    Than that, which one day worms may chance refuse?

In rejecting secular love poetry he of course rejects Venus, and God's dove will always outstrip winged Cupid in flight. There also seems to be an early favouring of simplicity indicated in the line "Will not a verse run smooth that bears thy name!" but Herbert himself is far from demonstrating any such thing here, and there is in contrast a good deal of showing-off in those first three lines.

Herbert decided not to include these two sonnets in *The Temple* and that is understandable. They have been called arrogant and self-righteous, but he was seventeen – an age at which one is almost expected to be arrogant – and they are remarkably accomplished for someone so young, and a very early indication of his technical ability.

'Sonnet II' follows much the same theme, but contains an interesting pair of lines:

Roses and lilies speak thee; and to make
A pair of cheeks of them, is thy abuse.

At first glance we might mistake this for the standard usage we find in such sonnet sequences as Sidney's *Astrophel and Stella*:

O tears! no tears, but rain from Beauty's skies,
Making those lilies and those roses grow

(Sonnet 100, 1-2)

But when Herbert says they "speak of thee", he is referring to The Song of Songs 2:1 "I am the rose of Sharon, and the lily of the valleys", and that the use of such words in secular love poetry is to debase them. It is this incorporating words from the Bible in his very earliest verses which is worth noting.

Two later poems – both bearing the title 'Jordan' – are often regarded as voicing his literary manifesto.

Jordan I

Who says that fictions only and false hair
Become a verse? Is there in truth no beauty?
Is all good structure in a winding stair?
May no lines pass, except they do their duty
    Not to a true, but painted chair?

Is it no verse, except enchanted groves
And sudden arbours shadow coarse-spun lines?
Must purling streams refresh a lover's loves?
Must all be veiled, while he that reads, divines,
    Catching the sense at two removes?

Shepherds are honest people; let them sing:
Riddle who list, for me, and pull for Prime:
I envy no man's nightingale or spring;
Nor let them punish me with loss of rhyme,
    Who plainly say, *My God, My King.*

Just as he had rejected Venus and Cupid, so here he rejects Hippocrene, the fountain of the Muses on Mount Helicon, and chooses instead the River Jordan, where Christ was baptised. In his opposition to secular love-poetry (*false hair*) and to the fashion for pastoral allegory (*enchanted groves*) Herbert is contrasting these *fictions* with the truths of religion. "Is there in truth no beauty?" he asks. And in the last line of the first stanza he even appears to be dismissing poetry altogether. It is there in that curious word *chair*. Plato, in *Republic 10*, had famously used an item of furniture – a bed – (but that would have been totally inappropriate in this context) in his argument distinguishing between the *essence*, the Platonic 'idea' of a thing, the thing itself, and then an artistic representation of that thing, in order to show that art is always two removes away from truth.

The "winding stair" is clearly a protest against complexity and the closing lines of stanza two are often read as being a further attack of the obscurities of metaphysical poetry as seen in Donne and later in Crashaw. Herbert's own poem, it has to be said, is again far from being simple and straightforward, but it has none of that chop-logic cheekiness of 'The Flea' or the strenuous intellectual demands made by 'A Nocturne Upon Saint Lucy's Day'. The final lines would seem to be arguing that complexities of this nature are totally outweighed by such a simple statement (borrowed from the Psalms) as *My God, My King.*

While 'Jordan I' is largely concerned with themes – the externals, one might say, of poetry – 'Jordan II' looks more closely at the creative process.

Jordan II

When first my lines of heav'nly joys made mention,
Such was their lustre, they did so excel,
That I sought out quaint words, and trim invention;
My thoughts began to burnish, sprout, and swell,
Curling with metaphors a plain intention,
Decking the sense, as if it were to sell.

Thousands of notions in my brain did run,
Off'ring their service, if it were not sped:
I often blotted what I had begun;
This was not quick enough, and that was dead.
Nothing could seem too rich to clothe the sun,
Much less those joys which trample on his head.

As flames do work and wind, when they ascend,
So did I weave my self into the sense.
But while I bustled, I might hear a friend
Whisper, *How wide is all this long pretence!*
There is in love a sweetness ready penned:
Copy out only that, and save expense.

At the outset we find him confessing that there was a time when he was as guilty as anyone of the extravagantly decorative style of the age. "I sought out quaint words and trim invention". (*Quaint*, as we have seen, was the word Coleridge was later to use of him.) And the line itself links him again with his illustrious ancestor Sir Philip Sidney, who, in line five of the opening sonnet of his sequence *Astrophel and Stella* had written, "I sought fit words to paint the blackest face of woe". Herbert partially justifies all this *burnishing* and *curling* by suggesting that God deserves no less. "Nothing could seem too rich to clothe the sun" (l.11) but Psalm 104:2 tells us that God is already decked "with light as with a garment" so none of it has been necessary.

Sidney, unable to find the right words he needed, had concluded that opening sonnet with the words. "'Fool', said my Muse to me, 'look in thy heart and write.'" Words which were soon to become famous and here we have Herbert following him, when his friend whispers:

> There is in love a sweetness ready penned:
> Copy out only that, and save expense.

The difference though, and it is an important one, is that whereas Sidney was determined to depend on his own resources and his own emotions, Herbert declares that he will depend solely on the word of God – *a sweetness ready penned* – for his inspiration and the echoes of the Bible which are there throughout his work show that he meant it.

Looking back at the confession contained in the first two stanzas of this poem, one cannot help wondering if he was thinking of those 'hieroglyphic' poems of his which featured in Chapter Four. He did not reject them though, and unlike the *New Year Sonnets* they have their place in *The Temple*. Herbert never fully gave up on the belief that "Nothing could seem too rich to clothe the sun". It is one of those many dilemmas from which he never tried to hide.

In 'A True Hymn' he is again, like Sidney, struggling hard to write a poem.

> My joy, my life, my crown!
> My heart was meaning all the day,
> Somewhat it fain would say:
> And still it runneth mutt'ring up and down
> With only this, *My joy, my life, my crown.*

> (1-5)

He is getting nowhere and those grumpy low vowels in line four tell us all we need to know about his frustration. The problem is that he can't shut those six words out of his mind, but then in stanza two he learns to accept them.

> Yet slight not these few words:
>   If truly said, they may take part
>   Among the best in art.
> The fineness which a hymn or psalm affords,
> Is, when the soul unto the lines accords.
>
>   (6-10)

What he is re-confirming here is his dependence, as a poet, not on himself, but on God. As he says in the poem's last stanza:

> Although the verse be somewhat scant,
>   God doth supply the want.
>
>   (17-18)

Even accepting, however, that any words of God far outweigh his own, when he finds that he cannot write any of his own then he is quite despondent – *drooping and dull* – as he puts it in 'Dullness'.

> Why do I languish thus, drooping and dull,
>   As if I were all earth?
> O give me quickness, that I may with mirth
>   Praise thee brimfull!
>
>   (1-4)

Writers of love poetry seem to have no such problem.

> The wanton lover in a curious strain
>   Can praise his fairest fair;
> And with quaint metaphors her curlèd hair
>   Curl o'er again.
>
>   (5-8)

Even though, as we have already seen, they trade in *fictions*, while Herbert's lover has *all loveliness* and *all perfections*. But he doesn't blame God. In a delightful piece of self-mockery he admits that it is really all his own fault.

> Sure thou didst put a mind there, if I could
>   Find where it lies.
>
>   (23-24)

In a series of negations in 'The Quiddity' he seems, at first, to be dismissing poetry altogether as being of no value at all.

The Quiddity

My God, a verse is not a crown,
No point of honour, or gay suit,
No hawk, or banquet, or renown,
Nor a good sword, nor yet a lute.

It cannot vault, or dance, or play,
It never was in *France* or *Spain;*
Nor can it entertain the day
With a great stable or demesne:

It is no office, art, or news,
Nor the Exchange, or busy Hall;
But it is that which while I use
I am with thee, and *Most take all.*

The title suggests an unusual duality, as a *quiddity* can mean both the essence of a thing, or a quibble, and the poem proves to be questioning the value of worldly things as against that of spiritual things. Herbert *appears* at first to be favouring worldly things, but this is one of those poems in which there is a sudden change of direction and what has been dismissed is, in the final lines, given a value surpassing all that has gone before. What he ends by telling us is that when he is writing verse he is so close to God that he is very far removed from all the worldly things he has just listed.

But when we pause and look at the actual things he has listed, we notice that they constitute no simple generalisation of the *world.* They are very much a part of what would have been Herbert's *own* world, his own aristocratic and court background. The "gay suit" reminds us of one of the very few criticisms of Herbert that Isaak Walton included in his 'Life' " … his clothes seemed to prove that he put too great a value on his parts and parentage." He would have had his share of great banquets and we know, of course, that he played the lute. In stanza two we read of other fashionable pursuits, such as the Grand Tour of Europe and in stanza three there is a shift from the court to the City and the new money-men.

His rejection of these worldly things is, however, so brief, so perfunctory, that it seems to lack any strong conviction; something noticeable also in 'Frailty' where he claims to be rejecting *honour, riches, or fair eyes*, yet in doing so refers to them as *fair dust, Dear earth, and fine grass*, the adjectives suggesting that the world was far closer to him than he would appear to be claiming. But would we believe him if he led us to think that it was an easy thing giving up all the benefits his birth had brought him? The honesty of his personal insights is one of the sources of his greatness.

Changes of direction – second thoughts – are a feature of several of Herbert's poems. Second thoughts are, of course, not unusual; they are what occur to us while we are actually thinking, but when we come to express that thought, especially when we come to express it in writing, we omit the false starts, preferring what looks, perhaps flatteringly, altogether clearer, instantaneous and more logical. Herbert does not do this. Often we are spectators to a mind in process – a part of the honesty.

We see this in a curious poem 'Denial', which is an echo of those psalms of lamentation which bewail God's seeming absence. Psalm 102, for example, where David pleads with God, "Hide not thy face from me in the days when I am in trouble." When Herbert feels that God has hidden his face and abandoned him, then his verse, as he says, fails entirely.

> When my devotions could not pierce
> Thy silent ears;
> Then was my heart broken, as was my verse:
> My breast was full of fears
> And disorder:
>
> (1-5)

The poem itself is an extraordinarily skilful demonstration of this 'failure', having a chaotic structure and a fifth line which repeatedly fails to rhyme with anything else until we reach the very end when God grants his request, *Come, come my God*, and the fifth line then has a rhyme, which is in fact the word *rhyme*.

'The Forerunners' is a poem which goes even further along this road of seeming failure. It is an 'old-age' poem in which he is bidding a final farewell to the writing of poetry and doing so, not unlike Coleridge, in one of his finest poems. The *forerunners*, or *harbingers*, were court officials who went ahead into a town where the King and his entourage were about to stay and commandeered accommodation for them with a white chalk mark on the door. Here the white marks are Herbert's first grey hairs.

The Forerunners

The harbingers are come. See, see their mark;
White is their colour, and behold my head.
But must they have my brain? must they dispark
Those sparkling notions, which therein were bred?
      Must dullness turn me to a clod?
Yet they have left me, *Thou art still my God*.

                              (1-6)

They may have taken over almost everything, but, happily, the officials have left him his heart and the words *Thou art still my God*, which, as in 'A True Hymn', are seen as being enough.

Good men ye be, to leave me my best room,
Ev'n all my heart, and what is lodged there:
I pass not, I, what of the rest become,
So *Thou art still my God*, be out of fear.
      He will be pleased with that ditty;
And if I please him, I write fine and witty.

                            (7-12)

Stanza three is an echo of the 'Jordan' poems, as he claims to have rescued the language of poetry from the grip of secular love poetry, here dismissed as "stews and brothels".

Farewell sweet phrases, lovely metaphors.
But will ye leave me thus? when ye before
Of stews and brothels only knew the doors,
Then did I wash you with my tears, and more,
      Brought you to Church, well dressed and clad;
My God must have my best, e'en all I had.

                           (13-18)

But having seemingly advocated simplicity, that old dilemma reappears: "My God must have my best, ev'n all I had." One would not wish him to be consistent when he can give us verse like stanza four:

Lovely enchanting language, sugar-cane,
Honey of roses, whither wilt thou fly?
Hath some fond lover 'ticed thee to thy bane?
And wilt thou leave the Church and love a sty?
      Fie, thou wilt soil thy 'broidered coat,
And hurt thyself, and him that sings the note.

                    (19-24)

And in stanza five "Beauty and beauteous words should go together". But he ends by insisting that *embellishments* – the "lovely enchanting language", which he clearly likes so much – cannot ultimately improve on *Thou art still my God*.

Perhaps there was a time when the craft of verse did fail him for a while. It is a common enough experience, and if it did, then it came back to him as he records in 'The Flower'. His heart, he tells us, was "shrivelled". This does not refer merely to an inability to write; there is a feeling of despair, and sickness and grief here too. It is an emotional winter, and in a brilliantly sustained extended metaphor he compares his heart to a flower which shrivels in the cold, but stays alive underground as a bulb.

Who would have thought my shrivelled heart
Could have recovered greenness? It was gone
    Quite underground; as flowers depart
To see their mother-root, when they have blown;
       Where they together
       All the hard weather,
Dead to the world, keep house unknown.

                    (8-14)

And then it blooms again in spring, a resurrection, as it were, which Herbert identifies with:

And now in age I bud again,
After so many deaths I live and write;
   I once more smell the dew and rain,
And relish versing: O my only light,
       It cannot be
       That I am he
On whom thy tempests fell all night.

                    (36-42)

The important point, for the moment, in this important poem, is the incontrovertible fact that he did indeed "relish versing", a relish to be seen in the unparalleled feat that out of the 169 poems in *The Temple* 116 are in a stanza form which he himself invented and which he never used again, and out of the remaining 53 poems 15 are sonnets.

One aspect of this versatility which is sometimes overlooked is his ability to write hymns, though it is not an ability which should surprise us. Time and again the act of writing a poem is referred to as *singing*. In 'The Dedication' it is "who shall sing best thy name". As we have seen, many of his poems are based on psalms and in Donne's funeral service for Magdalen Herbert we learn that the family were accustomed to singing psalms together on Sunday evenings.

A hymn is not at all the same as a poem. It has different needs – an organ and a full-throated congregation are a help. On the page it is shackled somewhat. It must have a strict metre from which it must not deviate. The language must be simple and direct and the sense cannot be allowed to run over from line to line and certainly never over a verse.

'Praise II' is instantly familiar to us, beginning:

> King of Glory, King of Peace,
> > I will love thee;
> And that love may never cease,
> > I will move thee.

In this, and throughout the hymn, it follows the structure of the Psalms, which relied on a system known as *parallelism*, wherein lines are sung alternately by opposite choirs in a statement and response. For example, Psalm 117 reads in its entirety:

> 1. O praise the Lord, all ye nations: praise him all ye people.
> 2. For his merciful kindness is great toward us: and the truth of the Lord endureth for ever. Praise ye the Lord.

Compact and spare as a hymn should be, the contrasts are stressed in lines which rise and fall, assisted by the feminine rhymes in the shorter lines. T.S. Eliot rightly called this a work of "masterly simplicity".

Herbert's other famous hymn is called 'Antiphon I' and again we instantly know the tune, so much so that it is almost impossible to 'read' it. It demands to be sung.

Antiphon I

Chorus   Let all the world in ev'ry corner sing,
                        My God and King.

Verse   The heav'ns are not too high,
                  His praise may thither fly;
                  The earth is not too low,
                  His praises there may grow.

The parallelism is emphasised by the division of the lines into a *Chorus* and a responding *Verse* and the contrast between heaven and earth is established by the high vowel sound rhymes of *fly/high* followed by the lower vowels *low/grow*. This is followed by:

Verse   The church with psalms must shout,
                  No door can keep them out:
                  But above all, the heart
                  Must bear the longest part.

Chorus   Let all the world in ev'ry corner sing,
                        My God and King.

As well as in the church, the place for the singing of psalms is the human heart, which to Herbert was *The Temple.*

In 'Easter', he wrote:

        Awake, my lute, and struggle for thy part
                      With all thy art.

                                  (7-8)

For all that he may have had to struggle, it was an art which George Herbert unquestionably possessed.

6

Parables and Narratives

"a verse might catch him"

A brief glance in the direction of the great eighteenth-century hymn-writer Isaac Watts can tell us, by way of contrast, a great deal about George Herbert. For instance, these four opening verses to one of his hymns are not untypical:

> My thoughts on awful subjects roll,
>   Damnation, and the dead;
> What horrors seize the guilty soul
>   Upon a dying bed!
>
> Ling'ring about these mortal shores,
>   She makes a long delay,
> Till, like a flood, with rapid force,
>   Death sweeps the wretch away.
>
> Then swift and dreadful she descends
>   Down to the fiery coast,
> Among abominable fiends,
>   Herself a frightful ghost.
>
> There endless crowds of sinners lie,
>   And darkness makes their chains;
> Tortured with keen despair they cry,
>   Yet wait for fiercer pains.

The feminine pronoun only adds to the unpleasantness, and some of his hymns intended for children must have been very frightening for them.

> There is an hour when I must die,
> Nor do I know how soon 'twill come;
> A thousand children young as I,
> Are call'd by Death to hear their Doom.

It hardly needs to be said that Herbert could never have written such lines. The Dissenters' obsession with Death, Sin, and the Fear of Hell is totally foreign to him. When he addresses *Death* in his poem of that name his tone, rather than fearful, is dismissive:

> Death, thou wast once an uncouth hideous thing,
> Nothing but bones,
> The sad effect of sadder groans:
> Thy mouth was open, but thou couldst not sing.
>
> (1-4)

In one of his *Holy Sonnets*, 'Death, be not proud', John Donne had argued forcefully and confidently with Death, but retained, nevertheless, a tone of some respect, whereas Herbert's attitude is so casual and superior as to be almost contemptuous, and in line four he even mocks the old skeleton figure with its mouth hanging open.

The skeleton, as Herbert sees it, is what remains, what is left behind, on this side of death.

> For we considered thee as at some six
> Or ten years hence,
> After the loss of life and sense,
> Flesh being turned to dust, and bones to sticks.
>
> We looked on this side of thee, shooting short;
> Where we did find
> The shells of fledge souls left behind,
> Dry dust, which sheds no tears, but may extort.
>
> (5-12)

It is like an empty eggshell from which the fledgling has flown – the fledgling here being an image for the soul, which is now elsewhere. As Saint Paul said in 1 Corinthians 15:42, "So also is the resurrection of the dead. It is sown in corruption; it is raised in incorruption." That dust, these bones and sticks are the corruption which has been left behind.

Herbert is not concerned with theological abstractions. The images of the resurrection he gives us in the following stanzas call to mind Stanley Spencer's wonderfully cheerful painting *The Resurrection Cookham*, where the village folk clambering out of their graves don't look as though they have ever been dead.

> For we do now behold thee gay, and glad,
>> As at doomsday;
>> When souls shall wear their new array,
> And all thy bones with beauty shall be clad.
>
> (17-20)

The poem ends with the traditional image of death being no more frightening than going to sleep.

> Therefore we can go die as sleep, and trust
>> Half that we have
>> Unto an honest faithful grave;
> Making our pillows either down, or dust.
>
> (21-24)

The very domestic and comfortable image of the *pillow* is so characteristic of his way of thinking. There is no horror here, no fear of damnation. What we see is Herbert's total confidence in salvation, and with death playing so small a part in his writing, it comes as no great surprise to find that Hell hardly features at all. Yet, considering the sulphurous flames and pitchfork-wielding demons which were to dominate so much of Puritan thinking and preaching, it perhaps ought to surprise us. It certainly tells us a great deal about the man himself that in one of his rare references to Hell, in a poem called 'Time', he says:

> Who wants the place, where God doth dwell,
> Partakes already half of hell.
>
> (23-24)

God, for Herbert, is Love, and to be excluded from that love would be the worst of punishments, so much so that failure to love God would in itself be the worst of punishments for failing to do so. As he puts it in the closing lines of 'Affliction I':

> Ah my dear God! though I am clean forgot,
> Let me not love thee, if I love thee not.

Once again in this poem 'Time' is depicted as the cloaked figure with his scythe and once again he is mocked;

> Meeting with Time, slack thing, said I,
> Thy scythe is dull; whet it for shame.
>
> (1-2)

On this occasion Time has an answer:

> No marvel Sir, he did reply,
> If it at length deserve some blame:
> But where one man would have me grind it,
> Twenty for one too sharp do find it.
>
> (3-6)

It is not an answer which Herbert is prepared to accept however. With salvation firmly in mind and looking forward to an eternity in paradise, he tells Time, in an image which is again marked by its domesticity, that his scythe, once a "hatchet" and to be feared, is now "but a pruning-knife" and that:

> Christ's coming hath made man thy debtor,
> Since by thy cutting he grows better.
>
> (11-12)

Time, which was once an "executioner", is therefore now no more than a gardener, or:

> An usher to convey our souls
> Beyond the utmost stars and poles.
>
> (17-18)

So far so good. Herbert is winning the argument, but he decides to take it one step further and it proves to be a step too far. Thinking of paradise, he says, makes life here on earth seem too long; at which Time promptly turns the tables on him:

> Thus far Time heard me patiently:
> Then chafing said, This man deludes:
> What do I here before his door?
> He doth not crave less time, but more.
>
> (28-30)

Brief as this poem is, there is so much poetic skill on display here: the conversational ease of the dialogue, the mini-drama and the humour. The end surprises us just as much as it does Herbert. Yet it has been dismissed as 'whimsical', as if there were no place in religion for humour. It is surely meant to be whimsical, and to make us smile. Herbert never feels the need to moralise; his faith is far too strong for that.

For all their refusal to moralise, however, there is in both these poems a directness (which is not the same thing as simplicity) and a narrative quality which marks them out as having something of the sermon about them. As Herbert had observed in the opening stanza of 'The Church-Porch' "A verse may find him, who a sermon flies", and lively little sermons these verses are. We are again reminded of what he said about Christ's parables in *The Country Parson* (Chapter 23) " ... that by familiar things he might make his doctrine slip the more easily into the hearts even of the meanest." But their brevity is one of the strengths of these poem/sermons. Herbert was never at his best in poems which ran to more than forty or fifty lines and so it is rather worrying to remember his suggestion that an hour was the best length (a "competency" as he put it) for a sermon. Maybe even in Bemerton the congregation could be found "gaping and scratching the head". (Chapter 6)

'The Pilgrimage' is another instance of a sermon/poem, but one which this time is something of a disappointment, as in the inevitable comparison with Bunyan's *Pilgrim's Progress* Herbert's verses strike us as being rather dull. It is quite possible though that Bunyan, writing fifty years after Herbert's death, had read the poem and been prompted by it. It at least begins promisingly:

> I travelled on, seeing the hill, where lay
> My expectation.
> A long it was and weary way.
> The gloomy cave of Desperation
> I left on th'one, and on the other side
> The rock of Pride.
>
> (1-6)

The deliberately awkward syntax of that third line does recreate the difficulty of the climb, but why a *cave* of desperation and why a *rock* of pride? There is no necessity here; they might even be reversed with no great loss or addition to the meaning. Then on the pilgrim goes, through *Fancy's meadow* and *Care's copse*, abstractions which tell us nothing at all. There is no sense of place and no description and we realise that visualising things has never been one of Herbert's strengths. In his imagery, smell and touch are far more evident.

Reading 'The Pilgrimage' makes us also recognise that Herbert is not a discursive poet. He could not argue a case the way Alexander Pope does. Uncharacteristically, 'The Pilgrimage' is also a very gloomy poem, and Herbert is not a gloomy poet.

One of Herbert's great virtues as a religious poet is that he does have a sense of the comic, a dry sense of humour, far more so than Chapter 27 of *The Country Parson*, 'The Parson in Mirth' would have us believe: "[he] intermingles some mirth in his discourses occasionally". We know nothing of his sermons of course, but as far as his poems are concerned he was never guilty of that pious solemnity we find so often in the nineteenth century.

His poem 'Redemption' – and there could hardly be a more serious subject – comes across as the most light-hearted of parables. Herbert has picked on a potential pun in the title, as *to redeem* can also mean to buy back or in the case of land to repossess it, hence this religious poem is dominated by the language and vocabulary of commerce. The speaker, finding himself in financial difficulty, goes looking for his landlord to try to negotiate a new and cheaper lease:

> Having been tenant long to a rich Lord,
>   Not thriving, I resolved to be bold,
>   And make a suit unto him, to afford
> A new small-rented lease, and cancel th'old.
>
> (1-4)

An alternative word for a lease could of course be a covenant, and we, as readers, forewarned by the poem's title, realise that what we have before us in this gentle monologue is the New Covenant of which St Paul speaks in his Epistle to the Hebrews: the New Covenant whereby the Law of the Old Testament is replaced by the Grace of the New.

The tenant first goes to seek his Lord "in heaven at his manor", but he is not at home. He has gone, so his servants say, to finalise a deal "About some new land, which he had dearly bought/Long since on earth". We soon recognise that this Lord is Christ and that he has come down to earth to redeem mankind, and we notice the ambiguity of that word "dearly". But the tenant, this bumbling Everyman, goes off searching in all the wrong places:

> knowing his great birth,
> Sought him accordingly in great resorts;
> In cities, theatres, gardens, parks and courts
>
> (9-11)

And here we seem to be, not in Palestine, but in England, and beginning perhaps to feel an uncomfortable affinity with him. Are we really so superior? Do we manage to do any better?

So far, this sonnet, in which so much has been going on, has maintained a calm and leisurely pace, but then:

> At length I heard a ragged noise and mirth
>> Of thieves and murderers: there I him espied,
>> Who straight, *Your suit is granted*, said, and died.

> (12-14)

And there before our eyes is the Crucifixion itself: the thieves and murderers Christ died alongside, and most shockingly, and unexpectedly, the *mirth*. The tenant, even as he achieves his gaol, is speechless, but there is nothing he need say. Atonement comes, Herbert is assuring us, unsought and even undeserved. Again, what we are shown is the God of Love.

The "I" in this brief, but graphic monologue is clearly not Herbert himself, and this should serve as a warning when we come to consider his more 'autobiographical' poems, and yet it is never quite simple and straightforward. 'The Quip', which looks to be a similar allegory or parable, contains elements which do inevitably look to be personal.

The poem presents us, as in a masque, with a procession of worldly delights and temptations, as they come to jeer at the speaker for not joining in with them.

> The merry world did on a day
> With his train-bands and mates agree
> To meet together where I lay,
> And all in sport to jeer at me.

> (1-4)

First it is Beauty that jeers at him, then Money, then "brave Glory" and finally "quick Wit and Conversation". To every jibe he responds with "But thou shalt answer, Lord, for me", an echo of Psalm 38 where "they that went about to do me evil talked of wickedness" and the psalmist prays "thou shalt answer for me, O lord my God".

Initially these look to be fairly standard personifications, but stanza three invites us to look more closely.

> Then Money came, and chinking still,
> What tune is this, poor man? said he:
> I heard in Music you had skill.
> But thou shalt answer, Lord, for me.
>
> (9-12)

We know of Herbert's skill as a musician, and there is no *necessary* link between Money, chinking , tune and music. The jeering is not, we realise, generalised. These temptations can be seen as reflecting his own inner anxieties. Is he perhaps too taken up with aesthetic things? His birth and social status? Walton hinted as much and in stanza four there is an actuality about the image of "brave Glory" which could only have come from someone who had himself been on the receiving end of the haughty contempt it portrays:

> Then came brave Glory puffing by
> In silks that whistled, who but he?
> He scarce allowed me half an eye.
> But thou shalt answer, Lord, for me.
>
> (13-16)

And in stanza five, which points to his ability with language, it is unlikely that the sometime Public Orator of Cambridge could have used that word *oration* without being fully aware of what he was doing.

> Then came quick Wit and Conversation,
> And he would needs a comfort be,
> And, to be short, made an oration.
> But thou shalt answer, Lord, for me.
>
> (17-20)

The final stanza again shows us Herbert's complete confidence in the power and protection of God.

> Yet when the hour of thy design
> To answer these fine things shall come;
> Speak not at large, say I am thine:
> And they shall have their answer home.
>
> (20-24)

But why should God show us such love? As the psalmist asked in Psalm 8, "What is man that thou art mindful of him?" Herbert suggests some answers to this question in his poem 'Man'. Interestingly, the American essayist Emerson also provides an answer in the closing chapter of *Nature*, pointing to that:

> ... wonderful congruity which subsists between man and the world; of which he is lord, not because he is the most subtile inhabitant, but because he is its head and heart, and finds something of himself in every great and small thing, in every mountain stratum, in every new law of colour, fact of astronomy, or atmospheric influence which observation or analysis lays open. A perception of this mystery inspires the muse of George Herbert, the beautiful psalmist of the seventeenth century.

And he then quotes fives stanzas from 'Man', adding Plato's assertion that "poetry comes nearer to vital truth than history."

Herbert's poem is a celebration of man, so positive, yet so simple and again so domestic. We seem to be suddenly intruding on one of his conversations with God. It is as though he has just remembered something he had heard earlier in the day, a sermon perhaps, and turning to Him, remarks, in the most casual and friendly of tones:

> My God, I heard this day,
> That none doth build a stately habitation,
> But that he means to dwell therein.
>
> (1-3)

Well, who could argue with that? In this case, however, the *stately habitation* Herbert has in mind is Man, and in the following eight stanzas he outlines his evidence.

Of our position in creation, he writes, "For man is ev'ry thing,/And more", an assertion best explained by reference to one of John Donne's sermons in which he says that it is wrong to describe man as a microcosm of the world, rather he is a Mundum Magnun, "a world in which all the rest of the world is subordinate." As he puts it – and nothing could be more anthropocentric – "the properties, the qualities of every Creature are in man, the Essence, the Existence of every Creature is for man, so man is every Creature." The "more" which Herbert adds follows from man being the only creature capable of reason and speech.

Reason and speech we only bring.
Parrots may thank us, if they are not mute,
They go upon the score.

(10-12)

The only words that parrots can utter they have to learn from us first.
Then comes a depiction of man's physical perfection:

Man is all symmetry
Full of proportions, one limb to another,
And all to all the world besides.

(13-15)

which calls to mind the diagram drawn by the Roman architect Vitruvius, which shows a human figure within a circle within a square, thus being the measure of a universe of perfect proportions.

Man's intellectual ability is shown in his scientific discoveries – "His eyes dismount the highest star" – yet stanza five not only looks back to the rather old-fashioned four elements – air, earth, fire and water – Herbert even has it that "the earth doth rest, heav'n move", which, for a friend of Francis Bacon, is a curiously Ptolemaic belief. But there is in Herbert very little of John Donne's "new Philosophy" which "calls all in doubt". Doubt was not an issue for him and the universe he lives in is far more homely and comfortable than Donne's.

Nothing we see, but means our good,
As our *delight*, or as our *treasure*:
The whole is, either our cupboard of *food*,
Or cabinet of *pleasure*.

The stars have us to bed;
Night draws the curtain, which the sun withdraws.

(27-32)

It is a universe which still acknowledges its dependence on the facts of the book of Genesis:

Waters united are our navigation;
Distinguished, our habitation.

(38-39)

In *The Country Parson* (Chapter 23) he had recommended the herb garden rather than the apothecary's shop. "In the knowledge of simples, wherein the manifold wisdom of God is wonderfully to be seen, one thing would be carefully observed; which is, to know what herbs may be used instead of drugs of the same nature, and to make the garden the shop." and this is the theme of the next to last stanza.

> More servants wait on Man,
> Than he'll take notice of: in ev'ry path
>   He treads down that which doth befriend him,
>   When sickness makes him pale and wan.
> O mighty love! Man is one world, and hath
>   Another to attend him.
>
> (43-49)

We find this also in his 'The Author's Prayer before Sermon': "Thy hands both made us, and also made us lords of all thy creatures; giving us one world in ourselves, and another to serve us."

This being so, and proved by so many examples, surely it is a "stately habitation" in which God would want to live. This has been the direction the whole poem has been heading in and it concludes:

> Since then, my God, thou hast
> So brave a Palace built; O dwell in it,
>   That it may dwell with thee at last!
>   Till then, afford us so much wit;
> That, as the world serves us, we may serve thee
>   And both thy servants be.
>
> (49-54)

It is worth pointing out here that even in a poem with a stanza form as complex as this, of the nine stanzas only stanzas two and eight have the same rhyme scheme. The more familiar one becomes with Herbert, the more astonishing his sheer technical ability appears.

Similar in many ways to 'Man' is 'Providence', a poem which, according to Herbert's most recent editor, has attracted relatively little critical interest. This is no real surprise, as although it is a delightful poem, the delight stems from the fact that it is, frankly, something of an anarchic jumble. There is simply no way of guessing what is coming next, but that is possibly its charm.

In 'Man', as we have seen, Herbert noted that we are the only creature capable of speech, and here he suggests that "Beasts fain would sing" (9) but as they can't it is incumbent upon us to be the "Secretary of thy praise" 98).

> Wherefore, most sacred Spirit, I here present
> For me and all my fellows praise to thee:
>
> (25-26)

The eighteenth-century poet Christopher Smart shared the same belief, declaring in his hymn 'The Presentation of Christ in the Temple':

> I speak for all – for them that fly,
> And for the race that swim;
> For all that dwell in moist and dry,
> Beasts, reptiles, flow'rs and gems to vie
> When gratitude begins her hymn
>
> (41-45)

But whereas Smart clearly meant it and continued to praise God on behalf of all mute creation, Herbert soon drops the idea and reverts to another of the themes of 'Man'.

> Thou art in all things one, in each thing many:
> For thou art infinite in one and all.
>
> (43-44)

Then from this he jumps without any warning to that brilliant image of the Tempest:

> Tempests are calm to thee; they know thy hand
> And hold it fast, as children do their father's,
> Which cry and follow.
>
> (45-47)

The jumps are so erratic. This is followed by a sequence of stanzas about food – God having ensured, we are told, that every creature's individual needs were catered for prior to its creation.

> Nothing engend'red doth prevent his meat:
> Flies have their table spread, ere they appear.
>
> (53-54)

'Providence' has been compared with Psalm 104, that great psalm of praise, but instead of its conies, storks and lions, here we have pigeons and bees. In one stanza we have a mixture of sheep, trees, springs and clouds with no obvious connection between them other than that of a degree of contrast and circularity:

> Sheep eat the grass, and dung the ground for more:
> Trees after bearing drop their leaves for soil:
> Springs vent their streams, and by expense get store:
> Clouds cool by heat, and baths by cooling boil.
>
> (69-72)

The *baths* here are apparently hot springs which are made to boil by the pressure of the cool air at the earth's surface.

After a stanza on herbs, in which he wishes there was one to help him write poetry, he leaps to "And if an herb hath power, what have the stars?" And then from poison to ships. Indeed the stanzas in the middle section of this poem could be re-arranged and shuffled about and we would not know any difference. The oddest is:

> Light without wind is glass: warm without weight
> Is wool and furs: cool without closeness, shade:
> Speed without pains, a horse: tall without height,
> A servile hawk: low without loss, a spade.
>
> (101-104)

It reads like a series of riddles, reminding us of Herbert's "hieroglyphic" poems and of his love of proverbs.

Even the versification of this poem is odd, with far more run-on lines than is usual with Herbert and some curiously strangled syntax. There are moments when it is hard to know what he can have been thinking about.

> How harsh are thorns to pears! and yet they make
> A better hedge, and need less reparation.
> How smooth are silks compared with a stake,
> Or with a stone! yet make no good foundation.
>
> (121-124)

But it is the complete unexpectedness of the poem which fascinates us, together with the occasional gem like the tempest image and lines such as:

> Most things move th'under jaw; the Crocodile not
>
> (139)

Not a fact we are likely to have realised until Herbert points it out. And there is the line coming after the revelation about the crocodile where he tells us that:

> Most things sleep lying; th'Elephant leans or stands.
>
> (140)

This curious belief that elephants could not kneel goes back a long way. Shakespeare believed it. In *Troilus and Cressida*, Ulysses, referring to Achilles' refusal to "bend" says, "The elephant hath joints but not for courtesy." And a hundred years after Herbert, when Christopher Smart wrote in one of his Seatonian poems, "Bow down, ye elephants, submissive bow", a reviewer soon put him straight. "Elephants cannot kneel", he was emphatically informed.

So varied and so uncertain of direction is this poem that it has even been suggested that the last two stanzas were each meant to be the final one and that Herbert failed to make up his mind!

It is not impossible that this seeming disorder is intentional. Having displayed such skill everywhere, why should Herbert not try his hand at anarchy for once? After all, the aerial courtship display of the raven, a master of flight, consists of pretending that he can't do it: he stalls and tumbles down almost to the ground. On the other hand, it *could* be seen to be representative of the variety of creation. Whichever, 'Providence' remains an unforgettable poem and is a tribute to "the wonderful providence and thrift of the great householder of the world." (*The Country Parson*, Ch 10)

7

The Passion

"for his enemies he died"

To write only religious verse is already to work within rather tight limitations, yet Herbert chose to narrow these limitations even further. There are events and issues central to Christian belief about which he has little or nothing to say, and that includes The Nativity.

There is one poem with the title 'Christmas' (though in effect it is two poems) and at the outset, the first sonnet, seems to be in a similar vein to 'Redemption', in that it tells a story. The story-teller has been out riding one day and as he and his horse are both tired he seeks lodging at an inn where he finds:

> My dearest Lord, expecting till the grief
> Of pleasures brought me to him, ready there
> To be all passengers' most sweet relief
>
> (6-8)

But even though there is mention of a manger, this is not the story of a baby or of a Nativity. The "dearest Lord" to whom he prays is already the adult Christ. What follows this sonnet, and reads like a separate poem, begins, "The shepherds sing; and shall I silent be?" It could be referring to the shepherds who were "abiding in the field", but it seems equally reminiscent of one of the singing contests of classical pastoral. As we have seen, Herbert knew how to write hymns, but neither of these sections would impress at a Carol Service.

In 'Whitsunday' there is some confusion and Herbert seems almost to be denying the existence of the Holy Spirit, or at least questioning its efficacy in the seventeenth century. And 'Trinity Sunday', which was considered in Chapter four, is a poem in which Herbert chooses to play intricate verbal and numerological games with various trinities (Faith, Hope and Charity etc.) but says nothing at all about the Holy Trinity.

What mostly occupied Herbert's religious thinking and much of his finest poetry is The Passion. Its importance to him can be gauged by the major part it plays in his 'The Author's Prayer before Sermon'.

> Thy hast exalted thy mercy above all things and hast
> made our salvation, not our punishment, thy glory: so
> that then where sin abounded, not death, but grace
> superabounded; accordingly, when we had sinned
> beyond any help in heaven or earth, then thou said, Lo,
> I come! then did the Lord of Life, unable himself to
> die, contrive to do it. He took flesh, he wept, he
> died; for his enemies he died; even for those that
> derided him then, and still despise him.

The last two lines of 'The Altar', a poem also looked at in Chapter Four, had read:

> O let thy blessed SACRIFICE be mine,
> And sanctify this ALTAR to be thine.

What follows after this is 'The Sacrifice' in which Herbert pledges that the sacrifice to be offered up on the altar of his verse will be Christ's Passion.

It is a long poem of sixty-three stanzas, each one being an iambic triplet followed by the refrain "Was ever grief like mine?" and it is spoken entirely by Christ. There is a long tradition of 'Complaint of Christ' monologues, many being Latin hymns, and in this country it can be traced back to the Old English poem 'The Dream of the Rood'. Herbert's poem is in this tradition, but also follows the example of the *Improperia*, or *Reproaches from the Cross* which are defined in the Catholic Encyclopaedia as:

> … the reproaches which in the liturgy of the Office of Good Friday the
> Saviour is made to utter against the Jews, who, in requital for all the
> Divine favours and particularly for the delivery from the bondage of
> Egypt and safe conduct into the Promised Land, inflicted on Him the
> ignominies of the Passion and a cruel death.

These *Reproaches* contain the repeated phrase: "My people, My people what have I done to you, how have I offended you? Answer me!"

The first stanza of Herbert's poem reads:

> *O, all ye,* who pass by, whose eyes and mind
> To worldly things are sharp, but to me blind;
> To me, who took eyes that I might you find:
>> Was ever grief like mine?

The opening words, as Herbert could and would have expected his contemporary readers to recognise, come directly from Lamentations 1:12. "Is it nothing to you, all ye that pass by? behold and see if there be any sorrow like unto my sorrow, which is done unto me". In fact there is not a single stanza of the whole of the sixty-three which does not echo or refer to some verse from the Bible.

Throughout the poem, each stanza begins with an initial statement which tells us what Christ has suffered, what has been done *to* him, and this is then followed by a related, yet contrasting statement, telling what he has done *for* his people and *for* the world. For example, Judas:

> For thirty pence he did my death devise,
> Who at three hundred did the ointment prize,
> Not half so sweet as my sweet sacrifice:
>> Was ever grief like mine?
>>> (17-19)

Before his betrayal of Jesus, Judas had objected to the waste of a precious ointment by Mary Magdalene when she anointed Christ's feet with it, and complained, "Why was not this ointment sold for three hundred pence, and given to the poor" (John 12:5)

The refrain inevitably breaks into whatever narrative momentum the poem might otherwise have achieved and we are tempted when reading to miss it out. This does obviate some of the monotony, but would clearly be going against Herbert's intention.

From the first mention of Judas, the narrative follows the events of The Passion in some detail, and largely as it is told in Mark's Gospel.

> Arise, arise, they come. Look how they run.
> Alas! what haste they make to be undone!
> How with their lanterns do they seek the sun!
>> Was ever grief like mine?

> With clubs and staves they seek me, as a thief,
> Who am the way of truth, the true relief;
> Most true to those, who are my greatest grief:
>   Was ever grief like mine?
>
> *Judas*, dost thou betray me with a kiss?
> Canst thou find hell about my lips? and miss
> Of life, just at the gates of life and bliss?
>   Was ever grief like mine?
>   (33-44)

There is a flatness in the telling which I do not think is helped by the continuous present tense and it soon begins to seem as though the sequence of events is being plodded through simply because it has to be. Nothing can be left out, but no one thing ever seems to be any more grievous to the speaker than another: the buffeting, the crown of thorns, the choosing of Barabas, fainting under the weight of the cross, the hammering in of the nails and the moment of death. It is all narrated in the same flat tone, until the final lines where the refrain is changed.

> But now I die; now all is finished,
> My woe, man's weal: and now I bow my head.
> Only let others say, when I am dead,
>   Never was grief like mine.
>   (249-252)

There are some stanzas where the parallel statement shows some ingenuity:

> Behold, they spit on me in scornful wise,
> Who by my spittle gave the blind man eyes,
> Leaving his blindness to my enemies:
>   Was ever grief like mine?
>   (133-136)

The spittle here is a reference to the curing of the blind man in Mark 8:23 "And he took the blind man by the hand, and led him out of the town; and when he had spit on his eyes, and put his hands upon him … and he was restored, and saw every man clearly." But such stanzas are few and hardly enough to raise our level of attention. W.H. Auden, again seemingly out of step with all other commentators, called it Herbert's "greatest poem", but then he also admired 'The Church-Porch'.

Following on from 'The Sacrifice' we have 'The Thanksgiving', a poem which can be read as a response to Christ's question "Was ever grief like mine?", and as instituting a sequence which will end with 'Easter'. It begins by addressing Christ as "King of grief" and asks the question, "How shall I grieve for thee?" (3) Thinking about it, Herbert decides initially that there is no way that he can adequately express such grief. Were he himself to weep blood and to be scourged, he could never equal the suffering undergone by Christ. But this is one of those poems which show us the mind in the actual process of thinking with all the changes of direction which that entails, and after wondering how he could ever manage to *imitate* Christ (15), he switches to what looks like a direct challenge.

> Surely I will revenge me on thy love,
>   And try who shall victorious prove.
>
> (17-18)

And the tone of the poem changes here too; it becomes boisterous and curiously smug. If he is granted wealth, then he will give it to the poor. Honour? Then he will honour God more. He will not marry, but if he does (consistency is not one of his strong points) he will offer up his wife and children to God. He will endow a chapel. Having gone through this list, it occurs to him that it is Christ's Passion he is supposed to be considering, but he puts that aside for a moment.

> As for thy passion – But of that anon,
>   When with the other I have done.
>
> (29-30)

And he goes back to his proposed good works. He will build a hospital and have the roads mended, but then, as if remembering that good works are never enough, he considers retiring from the world altogether. The he offers up, (and not for the first time, as we have seen) his skill in music and his *wit* and it seems here that he is referring to the poem which he is at this moment writing.

> If thou shalt give me wit, it shall appear,
>   If thou hast giv'n it me, 'tis here.
>
> (43-44)

Maybe he will simply read the Bible, and at this there is an unexpected note of triumph, as though he has won the challenge he proposed.

O my dear Saviour, Victory!

(48)

No sooner has he claimed a victory though than the Passion leaps back into his mind and in a totally unexpected reversal he realises that all he has been boasting of is totally inadequate. Suddenly he finds himself speechless. There is nothing he has to offer which could even begin to repay that debt, except perhaps humility, which is the note on which this remarkable poem now ends.

Then for thy passion – I will do for that
Alas, my God, I know not what.

(49-50)

But later, having given some serious thought to the matter, he follows with 'The Reprisal', which in an earlier manuscript had had the title 'The Second Thanksgiving'.

The Reprisal

I have considered it, and find
There is no dealing with thy mighty passion:
For though I die for thee, I am behind;
    My sins deserve the condemnation.

O make me innocent, that I
May give a disentangled state and free:
And yet thy wounds still my attempts defy,
    For by thy death I die for thee.

Ah! was it not enough that thou
By thy eternal glory didst outgo me?
Couldst thou not grief's sad conquests me allow,
    But in all vict'ries overthrow me?

Yet by confession will I come
Into the conquest. Though I can do nought
Against thee, in these I will overcome
    The man, who once against thee fought.

The new title was an astute after-thought, as a reprisal is a military term meaning retaliation and so takes up the "revenge" and "Victory!" of the earlier poem, but it is also a term used in music, a *reprise*, which means a return to the original theme, the theme of the Passion, and as he had said, "My music shall find thee."

For all that he has given more thought to the matter, Herbert is still no nearer to a solution to that first question, "How shall I grieve for thee?" and he admits that, "There is no dealing with thy mighty passion". Even if he were to go to the extremes of dying for Christ, he would, because of his sins, still be "behind" in the "dealing" and "deserve the condemnation." Herbert continues to write of it as a contest – hence the title 'The Reprisal' and he is not giving in yet.

The word "disentangled" in the second stanza is best explained by a line in 'Affliction I' "I was entangled in a world of strife". He is asking for innocence, forgiveness, but that would not be enough. He would still be behind, as it is only through the redemption, that is the strength given to him by Christ's death, that he could die for Christ. It seems to him to be such an unfair contest. Christ has always had the advantage of being divine, so could He not at least have let Herbert suffer more? It is an odd line of thought, but hopeless arguments with God are not at all unusual in Herbert's work and this one allows him to introduce a new approach by which he is determined to score some points. By *confession* he will defeat that side of himself which was once in opposition to Christ, that is his old, unredeemed self. The "old man" is the way Paul expresses it in Colossians 3: 9-10, " ... ye have put off the old man with his deeds; and have put on the new man, which is renewed in knowledge after the image of him that created him." The ineffectiveness of deeds alone was made clear in 'The Thanksgiving'.

This reference to *confession*, coming so early in *The Temple*, is a pointer to those personal and autobiographical poems which are generally regarded as being among Herbert's finest, and which will be considered in the next chapter.

On the Monday before Easter the Old Testament reading at Communion is from Isaiah 63:2 "Wherefore art though red in thine apparel, and thy garments like him that treadeth in the winevat?" In John 15:11 Christ is "the true vine", and these two readings combined to make the winepress, as it is depicted in medieval books of hours, an emblem of the Passion. This torture – the wringing out of Christ's blood – is the central image of 'The Agony'.

The Agony

Philosophers have measured mountains,
Fathomed the depths of seas, of states, and kings,
Walked with a staff to heav'n, and traced fountains:
    But there are two vast, spacious things,
The which to measure it doth more behove:
Yet few there are that sound them: Sin and Love.

Who would know Sin, let him repair
Unto Mount Olivet; there shall he see
A man so wrung with pains, that all his hair,
    His skin, his garments bloody be.
Sin is that press and vice, which forceth pain
To hunt his cruel food through ev'ry vein.

Who knows not Love, let him assay
And taste that juice, which on the cross a pike
Did set again abroach; then let him say
    If ever he did taste the like.
Love is that liquor sweet and most divine,
Which my God feels as blood; but I as wine.

The poem begins by encouraging an intellectual approach to Sin and Love. They should be investigated, explored and measured in accordance with the scientific spirit of the times. Herbert, we remember, was a friend of Francis Bacon. But then it tells us that to understand Sin we should to go the Mount of Olives, where Sin is what caused that agony and that shedding of blood, and to understand Love we should then go to Golgotha where Love is that blood itself. So Sin and Love are not the total opposites we might expect; they are correlatives, in fact identical, as each image is that of Christ shedding blood. There is a grim physicality in stanza two where the "press" is clearly an instrument of torture and pain is said to go hunting through every vein. The physicality of stanza three is no less, and yet is quite different, as it is something we must experience and is, one might say, distasteful, as in it we are being urged to drink the blood flowing out of Christ's pierced side. It is, of course, a reversal of the Eucharist, an inversion of the doctrine of transubstantiation; the blood in those closing lines has become wine.

Each of the stanzas in the next poem, 'Good Friday', is in the shape of a cross and there are five stanzas: the same number as the wounds that Christ suffered on the cross. It is also seen to be a poem about counting.

Good Friday

O my chief good,
How shall I measure out thy blood?
How shall I count what thee befell,
       And each grief tell?

Shall I thy woes
Number according to thy foes?
Or, since one star showed thy first breath,
       Shall all thy death?

Or shall each leaf,
Which falls in Autumn, score a grief?
Or cannot leaves, but fruit, be sign
       Of the true vine?

Then let each hour
Of my whole life one grief devour;
That thy distress through all may run,
       And be my sun.

Or rather let
My several sins their sorrows get;
That as each beast his cure doth know,
       Each sin may so.

[In modern editions these lines are followed by a further twelve lines in regular quatrain form, but an early manuscript has them as a separate poem with a separate title, 'The Passion', which is how it is proposed to deal with them.

Herbert turns once again to the question posed in 'The Thanksgiving': "how shall I grieve for thee?" This time he sets himself the task of counting (*measure, count, tell, Number*) Christ's griefs, but nothing seems adequate: not the number of His foes, the stars in the night sky, the falling leaves in autumn, nor all the hours he himself has lived. Interestingly, running alongside these words for counting – and sometimes they are the *same* words – are terms relating to the writing of poetry. *Measure* can also mean rhythm or metre. To *tell* can mean to narrate. *Numbers* once meant verses, and a *leaf* can of course mean a page in a book. Herbert's ingenuity does sometimes seem to be beyond measure.

Having failed to reach a *score* (a word which can also mean to write) Herbert thinks that perhaps what he ought to be grieving over is not Christ's sorrows but his own sins, which are the cause not only of his own sorrows, but of Christ's too. The closing image calls to mind a line in 'Providence': "Since where are poisons, antidotes are most". This change of direction is another example of Herbert appearing to think things through *as* he is writing.

The *writing* theme is followed up in 'The Passion'. The most appropriate (*fitting*) "ink", Herbert says, in which to express Christ's agonies and sorrows is "blood".

> Since blood is fittest, Lord, to write
> Thy sorrows in, and bloody fight;
> My heart hath store, write there, wherein
> One box doth lie both ink and sin.
>
> (1-4)

He asks Christ to write on his heart as there is not only a plentiful store of blood there, but it is a box where "lie both ink and sin", so when sin reads of the many sufferings Christ has undergone it will fly away.

> That when sin spies so many foes,
> Thy whips, thy nails, thy wounds, thy woes,
> All come to lodge there, sin may say,
> *No room for me*, and fly away.
>
> (5-8)

But there is always the danger that sin may try to return and so Christ is asked to dwell in Herbert's heart forever.

> Sin being gone, O fill the place,
> And keep possession with thy grace;
> Lest sin take courage and return,
> And all the writings blot or burn.
>
> (9-12)

In neither of these two poems, even though each is called 'Good Friday', does Christ actually die on the cross. It is in the following poem, 'Redemption', which was considered in the last chapter, that the petitioner finds his Lord among "thieves and murderers" and before he even has a chance to put his request to him "'Your suit is granted,' [Christ] said and died." As has already been observed, it is not death, but atonement and the resurrection that moved Herbert most, and 'Easter' is a poem which rings out in triumph.

> Rise, heart; thy Lord is risen. Sing his praise
> > Without delays,
> Who takes thee by the hand, that thou likewise
> > With him mayst rise.
> > (1-4)

With its opening words echoing the opening words of the mass: *sursum corda*, "Lift up your hearts", its note of triumph is also reminiscent of Psalm 9-10: "Awake up, my glory; awake lute and harp: I myself will awake right early. I will give thanks unto thee. O Lord among the people."

The second stanza is Herbert at his most *metaphysical*, compact and complex.

> Awake, my lute, and struggle for thy part
> > With all thy art,
> The cross taught all wood to resound his name,
> > Who bore the same,
> His stretched sinews taught all strings, what key
> Is best to celebrate this most high day.
> > (7-12)

The cross, being wood, is equated with the lute, and Christ's stretched sinews (rather grotesquely it seems today) with its strings, the one teaching the other how to make the music which will "celebrate this most high day". But since, as it says in the following stanza, "all music is but three parts vied", that is that a perfect chord is a third, one more element is needed, and so this part of the poem ends:

> O let thy blessed Spirit bear a part,
> And make up our defects with his sweet art.
> > (17-18)

Just as with 'Good Friday', there is a second part, also in regular quatrains, and it too once had its own title. It reads like a response to the first part in that it is a song, perhaps intended to be *the* song which the earlier lines were preparing us for. It has the charm and simplicity of a folk song and is in total contrast to what has gone before. Its theme is a familiar one though: that no matter what we try to do to praise Christ and to express our thanks and gratitude, he always surpasses us.

I got me flowers to straw thy way;
I got me boughs off many a tree:
But thou wast up by break of day,
And brought'st thy sweets along with thee.

The Sun arising in the East,
Though he give light, and th'East perfume;
If they should offer to contest
With thy arising, they presume.

Can there be any day but this,
Though many suns to shine endeavour?
We count three hundred, but we miss:
There is but one, and that one ever.

This could conclude the sequence on Holy Week but there is still one more poem to come – the baroque magnificence of 'Easter-Wings', the poem which in the past earned him so much derision, but which is now regarded as one of his major achievements, and which ends:

Let me combine,
And feel this day thy victory:
For, if I imp my wing on thine,
Affliction shall advance the flight in me.

8

Confessions

"affliction shall advance the flight in me"

'Easter-Wings', as we have just seen, ends with the lines:

> For if I imp my wing on thine,
> Affliction shall advance the flight in me.

Evidently, at this time, *Affliction* did not simply have its present-day meaning of a "condition of great distress, pain or suffering". There would appear to be something beneficial in it, and we find John Donne writing in his *Devotions lxxxvii* that "affliction is a treasure", explaining that, "No man hath affliction enough, that is not matured, and ripened by it, and made fit for God by that affliction." And in *The Country Parson*, Chapter 15 Herbert himself referred to "the benefit of affliction, which softens and works the stubborn heart of man", both poets no doubt recalling Isaiah 48:10, "I have chosen thee in the furnace of affliction". The importance of the word to Herbert is clear from the fact that he used it as the title of five separate poems, poems which tell of his anxieties and spiritual struggles.

The letter he wrote to accompany the manuscript of these poems, and intended for Nicholas Ferrar, had made the clearest reference to such struggles. It began:

> Sir, I pray deliver this little book to my dear brother Ferrar, and tell him
> he shall find in it a picture of the many spiritual conflicts that have
> passed betwixt God and my soul, before I could subject mine to the will
> of Jesus my master in whose service I have now found perfect freedom.

Affliction, therefore, consists of those *spiritual conflicts* which will eventually lead to *perfect freedom*. Another aspect, or consequence of affliction appears in 'Confession', a poem which begins with a truly metaphysical conceit, a totally unexpected blend of the domestic and the strange. The speaker, in an attempt to evade "grief", (and possibly God Himself) constructs a series of 'Chinese' boxes in his heart.

> O what a cunning guest
> Is this same grief! within my heart I made
> Closets; and in them many a chest;
> And like a master in my trade,
> In those chests, boxes; in each box a till:
> Yet grief knows all, and enters when he will.
>
> (1-6)

But grief, or affliction, cannot be escaped that easily, as we are told in another remarkable sequence of carpentry images:

> No screw, no piercer can
> Into a piece of timber work and wind,
> As God's afflictions into man.
>
> (7-9)

In the following stanza Herbert changes the metaphor and we are now *earth* and the griefs have become, "Like moles within us, [that] heave, and cast about". Trying to avoid them is no use. Paradoxically, "Only an open breast/Doth shut them out", and one way to achieve this is through *confession*. The importance of confession to Herbert is also there in Chapter 15 of *The Country Parson*:

> " ... in his visiting the sick or otherwise afflicted, he followeth the Church's counsel, namely, in persuading them to particular confession, labouring to make them understand the great good use of this ancient and pious ordinance."

The 1960s saw the rise in England and America of what became known as the 'confessional school' of poets: Lowell, Sexton, Plath, etc., but it would not be unreasonable to suggest that Herbert pre-dates them all, and especially with his honesty. For, as T.S. Eliot observed:

> "The great danger, for the poet who would write religious verse, is that of setting down what he would like to feel rather than be faithful to the expression of what he really feels. Of such pious insincerity Herbert is never guilty."

His honesty is apparent in 'The Pearl. *Matthew 13.45*'. The verses from Matthew refer to the familiar parable of the *pearl of great price*:

> 45. Again, the kingdom of heaven is like unto a merchant man, seeking goodly pearls.
> 46. Who, when he had found one pearl of great price, went and sold all that he had, and bought it.

It is a poem of renunciation and we must not forget that Herbert had a great deal to renounce, torn as he was between his religious calling and his secular ambition. In the secular world his aristocratic pedigree was impeccable. The Herbert family had distinguished itself along the Welsh Marches for generations. His elder brother, Edward Lord Herbert of Cherbury, had been ambassador to France. They numbered among their cousins the Earls of Pembroke and Montgomery. George himself had gained the notice and approval of the King when he was Public Orator at Cambridge. He had also served as a Member of Parliament. He knew his worth and there is no false modesty in 'The Pearl'.

Each of its first three stanzas begins "I know the ways ... " Later, these ways are called "labyrinths", a term of disapproval, as we learn from 'A Wreath', where Herbert confesses that God:

> knowest all my ways,
> My crooked winding ways, wherein I live,
> Wherein I die, not live: for life is straight,
> Straight as a line and ever tends to thee.
>
> (3-6)

The *winding ways* which he rejects in 'The Pearl' are those of learning, honour and pleasure. In the opening stanza it is not only the academic life of the universities he rejects, but legal and political learning too, and going beyond intellectual endeavour he rejects "Both th'old discoveries, and the new-found seas."

Success in the world of political and courtly intrigues would seem to have been as complex as the second stanza denouncing it.

> I know the ways of honour, what maintains
> The quick returns of courtesy and wit;
> In vies of favours whether party gains,
> When glory swells the heart, and mouldeth it

To all expressions both of hand and eye,
Which on the world a true-love-knot may tie,
And bear the bundle, whereso'er it goes:
How many drams of spirit there must be
To sell my life unto my friends or foes:
                    Yet I love thee.

(11-20)

He has been familiar, he says, with the quick wit and repartee of the court, the sexual liaisons and the skirmishing to win favours, skirmishes involving perhaps no more than a look or a gesture and so hardly apparent to an outsider.

Although the merchant in Christ's parable has here become Herbert himself, we notice the ingenious way in which he has managed to retain the language of commerce: *The quick returns, gain, to sell,* and *stock and surplus* of the previous stanza.

While his strictures against the academic world and life at court are not unexpected, what is unexpected is the way in which he rejects pleasure.

I know the ways of pleasure, the sweet strains,
The lullings and the relishes of it;
The propositions of hot blood and brains;
What mirth and music mean; what love and wit
Have done these twenty hundred years, and more:
I know the projects of unbridled store:
My stuff is flesh, not brass; my senses live,
And grumble oft, that they have more in me
Then he that curbs them, being but one to five:
                    Yet I love thee.

(21-30)

The total honesty here, the confession that "My stuff is flesh, not brass", gives us a very different picture of Herbert than some of his biographers have done. The Rev George Gilfillan, for one, must have chosen to overlook this stanza when he gave us his picture of Herbert as an undergraduate at Cambridge.

While many of his youthful contemporaries were engaged in riot, or "assembling themselves by troops in the harlots' houses," holy George Herbert sat alone and aloft in his evening chamber, with a musical instrument in his hand.

One cannot help being glad, for Herbert's sake, to have such a maudlin picture destroyed. There is even a degree of Keatsian lusciousness in those *lullings* and *relishes* and we know from his musical evenings in Salisbury that music and mirth went together. How could they not?

No matter what the attraction might have been (and he does not deny its appeal) in all this learning, honour and pleasure, it is negated at the close of each stanza by the same four simple words, "Yet I love thee", the stress falling, as we read them on *thee*. This is the one pearl worth all the others, a fact he makes clear in a final stanza which again takes up the language of trading and merchandise.

> I know all these, and have them in my hand:
> Therefore not sealed, but with open eyes
> I fly to thee, and fully understand
> Both the main sale, and the commodities;
> And at what rate and price I have thy love;
> With all the circumstances that may move:
> Yet through the labyrinths, not my grovelling wit,
> But thy silk twist let down from heaven to me;
> Did both conduct, and teach me, how by it
>   To climb to thee.

>   (31-40)

For all its honesty and direct personal reference, 'The Pearl' is written in what might be called Herbert's "plain" style. It does not – and this is the word he used so often when referring to poetry – *Sing*. We know that Herbert sang and that in his younger days his whole family would gather together on a Sunday evening and sing, but with the great age of hymn-writing still a century away, what they sang were psalms. Psalms would always have been an integral part of his daily worship throughout his life and their influence on his own poems is beyond dispute. He has in fact been called "a Christian psalmist".

Donald Davie's Penguin anthology, *The Psalms in English*, which includes versions by Wyatt, Milton, Vaughan and Smart, still gives us no more than a glimpse of the vast number of English translations that had been undertaken. It is estimated that over 260 complete versions were published between 1414 and 1862. Few, one would suppose, have much to commend them, but one of the most accomplished, and, for us, the most significant is that begun by Sir Philip Sidney and completed after his death by his sister Mary Herbert, Countess of Pembroke. Although not published until 1823, their work is known to have circulated widely in manuscript. Donne praised it and it is more than likely that Herbert, who was related to the Sidneys, had read it too. Indeed there are echoes and resonances enough to suggest that he had not only read it but learned from it. Davie has called the Countess "the first woman-poet of genius in the history of English poetry", pointing out that she hardly ever used the same stanza pattern twice, a technical challenge which, as we have seen, Herbert was to set for himself. There are certainly moments in her psalms which do call to mind Herbert's voice, and his liking for unusual shapes. For example the opening of her version of Psalm 139:

> O Lord in me there lieth nought
>   But to thy search revealed lies:
>   For when I sit
>   Thou markest it;
>   No less thou notest when I rise.
>   Yea, closest closet of my thought
>   Hath open windows to thine eyes.

When we listen to the singers of the Old Testament Psalter we hear so many different voices: bold and assertive, timorous and wheedling; and so many shifts and changes of emotion: anguish and triumph, joy and despair. And in Herbert's colloquies with God it is often these same pleas and remonstrations, celebrations and hymns of praise that we are hearing. The personal element in the psalms would have had a powerful appeal for him, but equally there is the drama, and it is this which made these centuries-old poems so much in tune with that particular aspect of metaphysical poetry, an aspect which is so evident in their liking for explosive first lines.

Psalm 38 begins, "Put me not to rebuke, O Lord, in thine anger: neither chasten me in thy heavy displeasure", and we are reminded of this as we read the first lines of Herbert's 'Discipline'.

> Throw away thy rod,
> Throw away thy wrath:
>   O my God,
> Take the gentle path.
>
> For my heart's desire
> Unto thine is bent:
>   I aspire
> To a full consent.

Not a word or look
I affect to own,
                But by book,
And thy book alone.

Though I fail, I weep:
Though I halt in pace,
                Yet I creep
To the throne of grace.

Then let wrath remove;
Love will do the deed:
                For with love
Stony hearts will bleed.

Love is swift of foot;
Love's a man of war,
                And can shoot,
And can hit from far.

Who can scape his bow?
That which wrought on thee,
                Brought thee low,
Needs must work on me.

Throw away thy rod,
Though man frailties hath,
                Thou art God:
Throw away thy wrath.

But there is an important difference between the psalm and Herbert's poem, for whereas the psalmist continues by heaping recriminations on his head, Herbert claims that even when he fails he is still doing his best. His God is not the fearsome God of the Old Testament and Herbert is not in the least afraid of Him. In fact he seems to be on such good terms with Him that he can go so far as to suggest that He has got it all wrong and that love would be far more effective than wrath. In the final lines he even seems to be reminding God that anger is a frailty and that He, as God, should be above such things. On the surface he seems to be remonstrating with God, but we sense all along that he is absolutely confident of His love and benevolence.

What he was not so confident of was his own worthiness to deserve such love and there are "confessional" poems which seem to reflect his years of uncertainty between 1624 and his ordination in 1630. He had taken minor orders after his year as a Member of Parliament, but there then followed prolonged periods of ill-health during which he appears to have doubted whether he was up to the calling and not, as some friends suggested, whether such a calling was fit for someone of his birth and social standing. We see these doubts and uncertainties in the two poems entitled 'Employment'.

In *The Country Parson* Herbert is adamant that idleness is "the great and national sin of this land" and insists that "fit employment is never wanting to those that seek it", but in 'Employment I' he seems to be rather less sure of this. Using the image of the flower – an image he turns to frequently – he is saying that seeking is not enough, that we have to rely on God's grace and hope that before we die – are "nipped in the bud" – he will *extend some good* to us. And even if we are so fortunate, we can make no claim for it ourselves, as the "sweetness and the praise" belong to God and then it will only be a *measure or* standard against which to compare the later joys of heaven which are the true essence, *The stuff*, in contrast to the things of the earth.

> If as a flower doth spread and die,
> Thou wouldst extend me to some good,
> Before I were by frost's extremity
> Nipped in the bud;
>
> The sweetness and the praise were thine;
> But the extension, and the room,
> Which in thy garland I should fill, were mine
> At thy great doom.
>
> For as thou dost impart thy grace,
> The greater shall our glory be.
> The measure of thy joys is in this place,
> The stuff with thee.

> (1-12)

But in our waiting we need not be idle; we can, and should, pray for God's grace.

Let me not languish then, and spend
A life as barren to thy praise,
As is the dust, to which that life doth tend,
But with delays.

(13-16)

Up to this point the poem has been, although by no means straightforward, somewhat drab and matter-of-fact, but the last two stanzas are Herbert at his finest. He is regretting his idleness. *All things are busy*, he says and recollects the flower of line one.

All things are busy; only I
Neither bring honey with the bees,
Nor flow'rs to make that, nor the husbandry
To water these.

(17-20)

It is in his simplicity that his power lies, especially when it is a simplicity as resonant as the final stanza.

I am no link of thy great chain.
But all my company is a weed.
Lord place me in thy consort; give one strain
To my poor reed.

(21-24)

Alone, as he sees it, in his *unemployment*, he has no part in the interconnectedness of things, the great chain of being. In terms of flowers, he is a *weed*. His prayer is that he might be permitted to join the *company*, the *consort*. And it is here that the resonances are heard. A *consort* can be a group of musicians. A *reed* is a weed, but there are also reed instruments on which a *strain*, or tune, can be played. But a *reed* can equally mean a pen and this last line might be referring to the poem which has just been written. When Herbert's verse moves onto a plane such as this, commentary of any kind can seem so superfluous.

In 'Employment II' he again gives voice to his frustrations. "He that is weary, let him sit," he begins. Clearly Herbert has no intention of just sitting still.

> He that is weary, let him sit.
>> My soul would stir
> And trade in courtesies and wit,
>> Quitting the fur
> To cold complexions needing it.
>
> (1-5)

The fur might simply be the warm clothing people need who simply sit around all day, but it might also refer to the academic robes he rejected in 'The Pearl'.

The poem proceeds in a series of images. At first it is the image of fire. Man is like a glowing coal and unless it is blown on it will go out. When the elements "did for place contest" fire rose up the highest while "The earth sat still". Life, he insists again, is "a business" (busy-ness) and the greatest of fires, the sun, shines perpetually "there or here", while the stars peep out only when it suits them. Then there is a jump to an image of busy-ness of a different kind altogether: the orange tree which bears blossom and fruit both at the same time. It is one of Herbert's most famous and most brilliant metaphors.

> O that I were an Orange-tree,
>> That busy plant!
> Then should I ever laden be,
>> And never want
> Some fruit for him that dressed me.
>
> (21-25)

An eminently practical man, as *The Country Parson* shows us, Herbert was well aware that we do not always want what we want once we've got it, and this applies not only to employment, but even – and such was his honesty – to the priesthood.

The Collar

I struck the board, and cried, No more.
                    I will abroad.
What? shall I ever sigh and pine?
My lines and life are free; free as the road,
        Loose as the wind, as large as store.
                        Shall I be still in suit?
        Have I no harvest but a thorn
        To let me blood, and not restore
What I have lost with cordial fruit?
                        Sure there was wine
Before my sighs did dry it: there was corn
            Before my tears did drown it.
        Is the year only lost to me?
        Have I no bays to crown it?
No flowers, no garlands gay? All blasted?
                    All wasted?
Not so, my heart: but there is fruit,
                    And thou hast hands.
        Recover all thy sigh-blown age
On double pleasures: leave thy cold dispute
Of what is fit, and not. Forsake thy cage,
                    Thy rope of sands,
Which petty thoughts have made, and made to thee
        Good cable, to enforce and draw,
                    And be thy law,
While thou didst wink and wouldst not see.
                    Away; take heed;
                    I will abroad.
Call in thy death's head there: tie up thy fears.
                    He that forbears
            To suit and serve his need,
                    Deserves his load.
But as I raved and grew more fierce and wild
                    At every word,
Me thoughts I heard one calling, *Child:*
            And I replied, *My Lord.*

The title can be read as referring to a clerical collar, or to a slave's collar, or even (one can never be sure with Herbert) to choler, or anger. The speaker is certainly in a rage and is determined to rid himself of whichever collar it is. It is a poem of rebellion and the opening lines sound like a teenager thumping on the table and threatening to leave home, but if this particular table is an altar, a communion table, as it seems likely to be, then it is a serious case of sacrilege that we are witnessing.

With its seven imperatives and its nine question marks, which might just as well be exclamation marks as no answers are called for, this is a very loud poem, and the verse form, which looks so anarchic on the page, is equally a sign of disorder. But it is a very deliberate disorder, for lurking among all this outrage and shouting we notice, if we listen carefully, a handful of words, *thorn*, *blood*, *sighs*, *tears*, *crown* which suggest the Passion, and *wine* and *corn* reminding us of the Eucharist. It is a very complex tantrum.

Up to the point where he asks is "All blasted? All wasted?" it has been one strident, unbroken dramatic monologue, but another voice is heard now. One might expect a second voice to provide a challenge against this outburst, to be the first speaker's 'good angel' in the debate, urging him to calm down and see sense; reason opposed to passion. But no. The first words we hear spoken by this second voice are:

> Not so, my heart: but there is fruit,
> And thou hast hands.

And this combination of fruit and hands tells us that this is a very bad angel indeed. Satan is urging him on in his rebellion:

> Recover all thy sigh-blown age
> On double pleasures:

The speaker needs no more urging. "Away" he says, "I will abroad". At this moment though he hears a very different voice calling to him. Has the title yet another possible meaning: *The Caller*?

> But as I raved and grew more fierce and wild
> At every word,
> Me thoughts I heard one calling, *Child*:
> And I replied, *My Lord*.

The rebuke is not simply because he has been behaving childishly; behind it is Christ's warning, "Whosoever shall not receive the kingdom of god as a little child shall in no wise enter therein." (Luke 18:17)

Herbert never pretends that faith is easy. As Chana Bloch puts it, "One of Herbert's great achievements as a religious poet is to reveal the "underside" of faith: the difficulty of holding on to what one most deeply believes."

In 'The Collar' we have referred to the *speakers*, but turning to the 'Affliction' poems there seems to be no doubt that these are autobiographical poems and that Herbert is writing of incidents in his own life and of his own feelings. This being so, what is surprising – shocking, one might say – is his blunt and forthright criticism of God in 'Affliction I'. Portraying Him as a master, Herbert accuses Him of a duplicity amounting almost to malice.

> When first thou didst entice to thee my heart,
> I thought the service brave;

he begins, and the connotations of that word *entice* suggest something not only sneaky but threatening; it is the paedophile with his bag of sweets. And this is followed by *entwine, betray* and *entangled.* Herbert has been seduced and trapped. At first, in his youth, everything went so well and he had no reason to doubt or to be suspicious of these *gracious benefits* (l.6)

> At first thou gav'st me milk and sweetnesses;
> I had my wish and way:
> My days were strawed with flow'rs and happiness;
> There was no month but May.
>
> (19-22)

We recall the wealth and social position he enjoyed, but the stanza ends:

> But with my years sorrow did twist and grow.
> And made a party unawares for woe.
>
> (23-24)

We might think of Job at this point, but at least God took some notice of Job and spoke to him. In this poem He is silent and Herbert makes no mention of his own possible sins and shortcomings which might have merited such woes. They are totally unexpected and – although he does not say so explicitly – undeserved. Among the woes which afflict him are sickness and we know that Herbert suffered prolonged bouts of ill health.

> My flesh began unto my soul in pain,
>> Sicknesses cleave my bones.
>>> (25-26)

And then:

> When I got health, thou took'st away my life,
>> And more; for my friends die.
>>> (31-32)

The death of the King in 1625, shortly after the decease of his two most influential patrons, the Duke of Richmond and the Marquis of Hamilton, had put an end to whatever political advancement he may have been hoping for and in a brilliant and characteristic image he tells us of his feeling of uselessness:

> a blunted knife
> Was of more use than I.
>> (33-34)

Academic success did come his way, but the words he chooses to record it are charged with negative vibes:

> Thou didst betray me to a ling'ring book,
>> And wrap me in a gown.
>>> (39-40)

Betray speaks for itself, but *wrap* seems more suggestive of a shroud than an academic robe.

In the tenth stanza we note a change of tense; it begins with the word *Now*. So far he has been looking back over the events of his life without much to cheer him and the present situation seems to be no better.

> Now I am here, what thou wilt do with me
>> None of my books will show:
> I read, and sigh, and wish I were a tree;
>> For sure then I should grow
> To fruit or shade: at least some bird would trust
> Her household to me, and I should be just.
>> (55-60)

If this image of the tree reminds us of 'Employment II', what follows recalls the closing lines of 'The Collar' as he declares himself determined to "seek some other master out". This time God does not intervene. He remains silent, but the enormity of what Herbert has just threatened pulls him up short and he does not need to wait for any word from heaven. Instead he speaks to God, and confesses, in a startling paradox, that if he does not love Him then he does not deserve to be allowed to love Him, which would be the worst of all possible punishments.

> Ah my dear God! though I am clean forgot,
> Let me not love thee, if I love thee not.
>
> (65-66)

In 'Affliction IV' Herbert does not accept this battering of woes so quietly. He asks God – indeed he sounds almost to be ordering God – to stop torturing him.

> Broken in pieces all asunder,
> Lord, hunt me not,
> A thing forgot,
> Once a poor creature, now a wonder,
> A wonder tortured in the space
> Betwixt this world and that of grace.
>
> (1-6)

That much of this opening stanza is indebted to the Psalms – 31:14 "I am clean forgotten, as a dead man out of mind: I am become like a broken vessel"; and 71:7 "I am as a wonder unto many" – makes it no less personal. This is not an outpouring of emotion. It is an analysis of a particular situation explored and explained through a series of images, with those of the second stanza providing readers with the greatest challenge.

> My thoughts are all a case of knives,
> Wounding my heart
> With scattered smart,
> As wat'ring pots give flowers their lives.
> Nothing their fury can control,
> While they do wound and prick my soul.
>
> (7-12)

The *case of knives*, an image in itself so typical of Herbert, is partly explained by a comment made by Walton in his 'Life': "He had a wit, like a pen-knife in a narrow sheath, too sharp for his body." Everything about him seems to be disintegrating and now even his thoughts cut into him, wounding both his heart and soul. The wounds are felt everywhere. They are *scattered*, like water coming out of the rose of a watering-can. The odd thing though is that such water gives "flowers their lives" and so seems to be in total contradiction to the life-threatening wounds. It may be that what is being said here is that afflictions of this nature can prove to be beneficial as is made clear in 'Affliction V' where Herbert says:

> Affliction then is ours;
> We are the trees, whom shaking fastens more,
> While blust'ring winds destroy the wanton bow'rs,
> And ruffle all their curious knots and store.
>
> (19-23)

But it is not only his thoughts that are letting him down. In the third stanza of 'Affliction IV' his "attendants", which we take to mean all his physical functions, are "quitting their place" and "Nothing performs the task of life". This time he turns to God for help, confident in his belief that with His help these woes will all be turned about and engaged to assist him in his quest for heaven.

> Then shall those powers that work for grief,
> Enter thy pay
> And day by day
> Labour thy praise, and my relief:
> With care and courage building me,
> Till I reach heav'n, and much more, thee.
>
> (25-30)

We are reminded again here of those crucial words in Herbert's message to Nicholas Ferrar, where he described his poems as "a picture of the many spiritual conflicts that have passed betwixt God and my soul, before I could subject mine to the will of Jesus my Master." And it is in 'The Flower' that this sense of the resolution of such conflicts, and of the new life which comes to him as a result, is given its most poignant expression. It begins by declaring:

> How fresh, O Lord, how sweet and clean
> Are thy returns!

And we notice that the word is in the plural – *returns*. There have been many such conflicts and many such resolutions and returns.

In poetry, the more usual direction of thought is from the physical to the spiritual. Some event or feature of the physical world suggests a spiritual parallel or connection, an activity evoking an inner experience, but here Herbert begins with the *returns* and then proceeds to explain them by way of *flowers*. In this way, as Alexander Pope points out, "New things are made familiar",

> How fresh, O Lord, how sweet and clean
> Are thy returns! ev'n as the flowers in spring;
> To which, besides their own demean,
> The late-past frosts tributes of pleasures bring.
> Grief melts away
> Like snow in May,
> As if there were no such cold thing.
>
> (1-7)

The eight strong monosyllables in the last line give it the emphasis of certainty. In stanza two he looks back to one of those occasions when he seemed to have lost God's love and when as a result his heart felt "shrivelled". It was like a bulb. When the leaves wither, it does not die but draws in its resources and waits for the return of next year's warmer weather.

> Who would have thought my shrivelled heart
> Could have recovered greenness? It was gone
> Quite underground; as flowers depart
> To see their mother-root, when they have blown;
> Where they together
> All the hard weather,
> Dead to the world, keep house unknown.
>
> (8-14)

In stanza three he makes clear the connection with the human situation and accepts that there are bad times, but rejoices that they do not last.

These are thy wonders, Lord of power.
Killing and quick'ning, bringing down to hell
    And up to heaven in an hour;
Making a chiming of a passing-bell.
        We say amiss,
        This or that is:
Thy word is all, if we could spell.

(15-21)

The funereal *passing-bell* can become the chimes of celebration and it is our own fault, our own ignorance, if we do not understand God's design.

His wish, nevertheless, in stanza four is that these changes cease to happen and that he could be forever in an unchanging paradise, but he acknowledges that his sins prevent this, try as he might, and that God's righteous anger is no less than he deserves. But then, in one of his finest stanzas, he considers the blessed state he finds himself in when his heart has recovered greenness once again. This joy is spiritual but it is also the joy of a poet – unquestionably Herbert's own joy – when he finds that the gift of words has come back to him. They are also the words of a poet who knows what sickness and recovery mean.

And now in age I bud again,
After so many deaths I live and write;
    I once more smell the dew and rain,
And relish versing: O my only light,
        It cannot be
        That I am he
On whom thy tempests fell all night.

(36-42)

It is courageous, to say the least, to disagree with both Coleridge and T.S. Eliot, but we do not need to share Herbert's religious beliefs to be able to admire and understand poems such as these, or to respond to the emotions which gave rise to them and which they in their own turn evoke. And it seems an appropriate moment, with this particular group of poems in mind, to recall those words of L.C. Knights, himself a non-believer, who put it so aptly when he wrote that they are "important human documents because they handle with honesty and insight questions that, in one form or another, we all have to meet with if we wish to come to terms with life." It is a statement which could not be simpler or more true.

'The Flower' has been called "one of the greatest lyrics in the language" and this is not a judgement one would wish to argue against, unless, that is, 'Love III' was being put forward as a contestant.

> Love bade me welcome: yet my soul drew back,
>> Guilty of dust and sin.
> But quick-eyed Love, observing me grow slack
>> From my first entrance in,
> Drew nearer to me, sweetly questioning,
>> If I lacked anything.
>
> A guest, I answered, worthy to be here:
>> Love said, You shall be he.
> I the unkind, ungrateful? Ah, my dear,
>> I cannot look on thee.
> Love took my hand, and smiling did reply,
>> Who made the eyes, but I?
>
> Truth Lord, but I have marred them: let my shame
>> Go where it doth deserve.
> And know you not, says Love, who bore the blame?
>> My dear, then I will serve.
> You must sit down, says Love, and taste my meat:
>> So I did sit and eat.

At one level this poem tells us a story in which a guest arrives at a feast, but is reluctant to go in because he is dusty and dirty from so much travelling, and anyway he feels that he is not worthy of such an invitation. The host gently insists and the guest agrees, but asks to be allowed to serve rather than to be served. This offer also is courteously brushed aside and at last the guest gives in and sits down to eat.

We soon realise of course that this is not *a story*. The host is called *Love* and the courtesy and kindness shown to the guest remind us of Paul's words in I Corinthians: that Love is *kind, suffereth long, doth not behave itself unseemly*, and so on. This and the simplicity and directness of the *story* suggest a parable, and point us particularly towards the parable of the marriage feast in Matthew 22 and the reluctant wedding guests. Added to this, the sensuousness and sexual ambiguities recall 'The Song of Songs'. 'Love III', as we have seen in so many of Herbert's poems, consists of layers of Biblical echoes and references. The guest's feeling of inadequacy is there, to give just one instance, in Exodus 4:10 when

Moses pleads that he is not eloquent, that he is slow of tongue, and God replies, "Who hath made man's mouth?", words which must have been in Herbert's mind in line twelve when Love asks "Who made the eyes, but I?"

But what is it a parable *of*? To some it tells of a Christian soul being received into heaven and as it is the last poem in *The Temple* it is seen as being a final resolution of all the conflicts we have been witness to: a reward such as Christ offered in Luke 12:37 "Blessed are those servants whom the Lord when he cometh shall find watching: verily I say unto you that he shall gird himself, and make them to sit down to meat, and will come forth and serve them."

Such a reading is not to be denied, but a further level is added if we recognise the poem's unspoken play on words whereby *host* is both the giver of the feast and the feast itself – that is the Eucharist. The guest insists that he is unworthy, a word we find throughout the Bible, but one which is used most significantly in the Communion prayer. "Lord, I am not worthy to receive you, but only say the word and I shall be healed."

This range of reference, coupled with such seeming simplicity, makes this discourse with God a quintessentially Herbertian poem. And it is generally agreed that it is one of Herbert's greatest poems. How, though, are we to account for its greatness? Consider the closing line: six unremarkable, one-syllable words; none of which carries any more stress than another. It is a line apparently devoid of meter, a line which deliberately refuses to call attention to itself.

So I did sit and eat.

Yet there is a finality to it, and a resonance, a resonance we would struggle hard to account for, but which we instinctively recognise as testimony of an exceptional poetic gift.

Bibliography

Editions

John Tobin, (ed), *George Herbert, The Complete Poems in English*,
  Penguin Books, 2004.
Helen Wilcox, (ed), *The English Poems of George Herbert*, CUP, 2007.

Biographical/ Critical

Chana Bloch, *Spelling the Word: George Herbert and the Bible*,
  University of California Press, 1985.
Margaret Bottrall, *George Herbert*, John Murray, 1954.
Amy M. Charles. *A Life of George Herbert*, Cornell University Press, 1977.
Marchette Chute, *Two Gentlemen*, Dutton & Co., 1959.
George L. Duyckincjk, *The Life of George Herbert*, Kessinger Publishing,
  2007.
T.S. Eliot, *George Herbert*, Longmans, 1962.
Jane Falloon, *The Heart in Pilgrimage*, Milton Keynes, 2007.
Jim Hunter, *The Metaphysical Poets*, London, 1965.
L.C. Knights, 'George Herbert' in *Explorations*, Chatto & Windus, 1946.
Cristina Malcomson, *George Herbert: A Literary Life*, Macmillan, 2004.
C.A. Patrides, (ed) *George Herbert: The Critical Heritage*,
  Routledge & Kegan Paul, 1983.
Arnold Stein, *George Herbert's Lyrics*, Johns Hopkins University Press, 1968.
Joseph Summers, *George Herbert: His Religion and Art*, Chatto & Windus,
  1954.
Rosemond Tuve, *A Reading of George Herbert*, Faber & Faber, 1952.
Helen Vendler, *The Poetry of George Herbert*, Harvard University Press, 1975.
James Boyd White, *The Book of Starres*, University of Michigan Press, 1994.

GREENWICH EXCHANGE BOOKS

STUDENT GUIDE LITERARY SERIES

The Greenwich Exchange Student Guide Literary Series is a collection of essays on major or contemporary serious writers in English and selected European languages. The series is for the student, the teacher and the 'common reader' and is an ideal resource for libraries. The *Times Educational Supplement* praised these books, saying, "The style of [this series] has a pressure of meaning behind it. Readers should learn from that … If art is about selection, perception and taste, then this is it."

The series includes:
Antonin Artaud by Lee Jamieson (978-1-871551-98-3)
W.H. Auden by Stephen Wade (978-1-871551-36-5)
Jane Austen by Pat Levy (978-1-871551-89-1)
Honoré de Balzac by Wendy Mercer (978-1-871551-48-8)
Louis de Bernières by Rob Spence (978-1-906075-13-2)
William Blake by Peter Davies (978-1-871551-27-3)
The Brontës by Peter Davies (978-1-871551-24-2)
Robert Browning by John Lucas (978-1-871551-59-4)
Lord Byron by Andrew Keanie (978-1-871551-83-9)
Samuel Taylor Coleridge by Andrew Keanie (978-1-871551-64-8)
Joseph Conrad by Martin Seymour-Smith (978-1-871551-18-1)
William Cowper by Michael Thorn (978-1-871551-25-9)
Charles Dickens by Robert Giddings (987-1-871551-26-6)
Emily Dickinson by Marnie Pomeroy (978-1-871551-68-6)
John Donne by Sean Haldane (978-1-871551-23-5)
Elizabethan Love Poets by John Greening (978-1-906075-52-1)
Ford Madox Ford by Anthony Fowles (978-1-871551-63-1)
Sigmund Freud by Stephen Wilson (978-1-906075-30-9)
The Stagecraft of Brian Friel by David Grant (978-1-871551-74-7)
Robert Frost by Warren Hope (978-1-871551-70-9)
Patrick Hamilton by John Harding (978-1-871551-99-0)
Thomas Hardy by Sean Haldane (978-1-871551-33-4)
Seamus Heaney by Warren Hope (978-1-871551-37-2)
Joseph Heller by Anthony Fowles (978-1-871551-84-6)
George Herbert By Neil Curry & Natasha Curry (978-1-906075-40-8)

Gerard Manley Hopkins by Sean Sheehan (978-1-871551-77-8)
James Joyce by Michael Murphy (978-1-871551-73-0)
Philip Larkin by Warren Hope (978-1-871551-35-8)
Laughter in the Dark – The Plays of Joe Orton by Arthur Burke (978-1-871551-56-3)
George Orwell by Warren Hope (978-1-871551-42-6)
Sylvia Plath by Marnie Pomeroy (978-1-871551-88-4)
Poets of the First World War by John Greening (978-1-871551-79-2)
Alexander Pope by Neil Curry (978-1-906075-23-1)
Philip Roth by Paul McDonald (978-1-871551-72-3)
Shakespeare's *A Midsummer Night's Dream* by Matt Simpson (978-1-871551-90-7)
Shakespeare's *As You Like It* by Matt Simpson (978-1-906075-46-0)
Shakespeare's *Hamlet* by Peter Davies (978-1-906075-12-5)
Shakespeare's *Julius Caesar* by Matt Simpson (978-1-906075-37-8)
Shakespeare's *King Lear* by Peter Davies (978-1-871551-95-2)
Shakespeare's *Macbeth* by Matt Simpson (978-1-871551-69-3)
Shakespeare's *The Merchant of Venice* by Alan Ablewhite (978-1-871551-96-9)
Shakespeare's *Much Ado About Nothing* by Matt Simpson (978-1-906075-01-9)
Shakespeare's Non-Dramatic Poetry by Martin Seymour-Smith (978-1-871551-22-8)
Shakespeare's *Othello* by Matt Simpson (978-1-871551-71-6)
Shakespeare's *Romeo and Juliet* by Matt Simpson (978-1-906075-17-0)
Shakespeare's Second Tetralogy: *Richard II–Henry V*
  by John Lucas (978-1-871551-97-6)
Shakespeare's Sonnets by Martin Seymour-Smith (978-1-871551-38-9)
Shakespeare's *The Tempest* by Matt Simpson (978-1-871551-75-4)
Shakespeare's *Twelfth Night* by Matt Simpson (978-1-871551-86-0)
Shakespeare's *The Winter's Tale* by John Lucas (978-1-871551-80-8)
Tobias Smollett by Robert Giddings (978-1-871551-21-1)
Alfred, Lord Tennyson by Michael Thorn (978-1-871551-20-4)
Dylan Thomas by Peter Davies (978-1-871551-78-5)
William Wordsworth by Andrew Keanie (978-1-871551-57-0)
W.B. Yeats by John Greening (978-1-871551-34-1)

FOCUS Series (ISBN prefix 978-1-906075 applies to all the following titles)
James Baldwin: *Go Tell It on the Mountain* by Neil Root (44-6)
William Blake: *Songs of Innocence and Experience* by Matt Simpson (26-2)
Emily Brontë: *Wuthering Heights* by Matt Simpson (10-1)
Angela Carter: *The Bloody Chamber and Other Stories* by Angela Topping (25-5)
George Eliot: *Middlemarch* by John Axon (06-4)
T.S. Eliot: *The Waste Land* by Matt Simpson (09-5)
F. Scott Fitzgerald: *The Great Gatsby* by Peter Davies (29-3)
Michael Frayn: *Spies* by Angela Topping (08-8)
Thomas Hardy: *Poems of 1912–13* by John Greening (04-0)